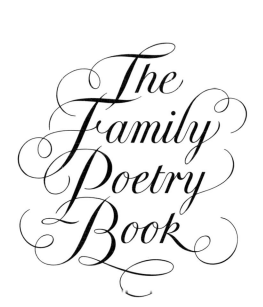

The Family Poetry Book

The Family Poetry Book

Foreword by
Felicity Kendal

MICHAEL JOSEPH
London

MICHAEL JOSEPH LTD
Published by the Penguin Group
27 Wrights Lane, London W8 5TZ England
Viking Penguin Inc., 375 Hudson Street, New York, New York 10014, USA
Penguin Books Australia Ltd, Ringwood, Victoria, Australia
Penguin Books Canada Ltd, 2801 John Street, Markham, Ontario, Canada L3R 1B4
Penguin Books (NZ) Ltd, 182–190 Wairau Road, Auckland 10, New Zealand

Penguin Books Ltd, Registered Offices, Harmondsworth, Middlesex, England

First Published in Great Britain September 1990
Second impression before publication September 1990
Third impression March 1991

Typeset in Linotron 10½ pt on 12½ pt Bembo by
Goodfellow and Egan Ltd, Cambridge
Printed and bound in Great Britain by Butler and Tanner, Frome, Somerset

A CIP catalogue record for this book is available
from the British Library

ISBN 0 7181 3456 7

All royalties from this book are to be donated to:

LEUKAEMIA RESEARCH FUND
43 Great Ormond Street, London WC1N 3JJ
Telephone: 071-405 0101

Contents

Note on the Selection of Poems

Each contributor was invited to choose their ten favourite poems. From the 400 or so selected between them, the top 100 were ranked by the following points system.

Where the poems were listed in order of preference, a number ten was given 11 points, a number nine 12 points, a number eight 13 points and so on, up to 19 points for a number two. Each number one poem was given 21 points. Where the contributors chose not to rank their top ten in order, the total number of points available, 156, was divided by ten and each poem was given 15.6 points. The top 100 are therefore the highest scoring poems. Since twenty-one poems contested equally for the last eleven places, eleven were chosen alphabetically by poet. (The other ten were 'Show Saturday', Philip Larkin; 'Halfway Down', A. A. Milne; Sonnet 66, William Shakespeare; 'The Child is not Dead', 'Tired with all these, for restful death I cry', Ingrid Jonker; 'When the hounds of spring are on winter's traces', A. C. Swinburne; 'Disabled', Wilfred Owen; 'Solitude', A. A. Milne; 'The Sunlight on the Garden', Louis MacNeice; 'Ode on Melancholy', John Keats; 'Ode to the West Wind', Percy Bysshe Shelley). Permission was not granted to include extracts from 'East Coker' ('So here I am, in the middle way, having had twenty years') and 'Little Gidding' ('In the uncertain hour before the morning') by T. S. Eliot, which would otherwise have been at places 33 and 64.

The poems are listed in order of popularity: hence, Andrew Marvell's 'To his Coy Mistress', first in the book, is the most popular poem. Brackets in the contents list indicate poems of equal popularity. Because of length, some of the longer poems are not quoted in their entirety. A list of each contributor's poems appears on pages 184–203.

Foreword

A shared love for particular poems – can there be a surer way of knowing one's truest friends and fellow spirits? The one hundred poems in this book make a kinship of you who find your best-loved poetry here and of those of us who helped to choose them. Yes, it is a *family* poetry book in more senses than one.

First and foremost *The Family Poetry Book* offers itself as a feast for everyone who loves poetry; and I hope it will establish itself as a favourite anthology to be picked up by those who like to come across an old friend, well-remembered or half-forgotten, or equally to make a new one.

But among the pleasures of this book, not least is the glimpse it gives us into the souls of the varied and distinguished contributors. When I compare the list of my own top ten poems with those of the other contributors, how can I help feeling a special bond with people who picked 'my' Shakespeare sonnet? And if ever my friendship with, and regard for, Anna Massey needed sealing, how can it not be sealed for ever when I see that she and I, together and alone, declared ourselves for W. B. Yeats's 'The Song of Wandering Ængus'? But perhaps *the* Yeats poem for you is 'Sailing to Byzantium' – in which case Martin Amis and John Carey agree with you. Or if you carry a torch for Yeats's 'The Second Coming', there you would be in the company of Denis Healey, Elizabeth Longford and Katharine Whitehorn. Another fascination in reading this anthology is in seeing how many of the hundred most popular poems were honourable near-misses in one's personal top ten; and how many of them hold out the possibility of becoming a new favourite.

Some of us had put forward poems by living writers, but you may notice that in those pages we are in the society of dead poets (John Betjeman and Philip Larkin being the last to leave us). So I ask myself whether we contributors are a backward-looking bunch, and whether we should account for ourselves.

Not really, I think. By its nature this is a book of poems which unite people and it takes time for poetry to do that, to prove itself as a poem not merely for you or me, but for generations. There are poems here which I heard for the first time from my parents, and which my two-year-old son will hear for the first time from me, and which I think and hope my children will one day read to their children. There will be other poems, too, of course, some still to prove their place, some still to be written. So it goes and so it should.

I hope you enjoy this selection, which has been made in what I believe is a unique way. Because so many temperaments have combined to choose the poems and because poetry appeals to so many different moods, you will find yourself in wonderfully varied company.

And of course it is important to add that this book gives us the opportunity to support a most deserving cause, the Leukaemia Research Fund, so let me add a note of thanks to the publishers, and I'm sorry I can't say it as a sonnet!

THE POEMS

To his Coy Mistress

HAD we but World enough, and Time,
This coyness Lady were no crime.
We would sit down, and think which way
To walk, and pass our long Loves Day.
Thou by the Indian Ganges side
Should'st Rubies find: I by the Tide
Of Humber would complain. I would
Love you ten years before the Flood:
And you should if you please refuse
Till the Conversion of the Jews.
My vegetable Love should grow
Vaster than Empires, and more slow.
An hundred years should go to praise
Thine Eyes, and on thy Forehead Gaze.
Two hundred to adore each Breast:
But thirty thousand to the rest.
An Age at least to every part,
And the last Age should show your Heart.
For Lady you deserve this State;
Nor would I love at lower rate.
    But at my back I alwaies hear
Times winged Charriot hurrying near:
And yonder all before us lye
Desarts of vast Eternity.
Thy Beauty shall no more be found;
Nor, in thy marble Vault, shall sound
My ecchoing Song: then Worms shall try
That long preserv'd Virginity:
And your quaint Honour turn to dust;
And into ashes all my Lust.
The Grave's a fine and private place,
But none I think do there embrace.
    Now therefore, while the youthful hew
Sits on thy skin like morning dew,

And while thy willing Soul transpires
At every pore with instant Fires,
Now let us sport us while we may;
And now, like am'rous birds of prey,
Rather at once our Time devour,
Than languish in his slow-chapt pow'r.
Let us roll all our Strength, and all
Our sweetness, up into one Ball:
And tear our Pleasures with rough strife,
Thorough the Iron gates of Life.
Thus, though we cannot make our Sun
Stand still, yet we will make him run.

ANDREW MARVELL

Ode to a Nightingale

 సOు

My heart aches, and a drowsy numbness pains
  My sense, as though of hemlock I had drunk,
Or emptied some dull opiate to the drains
  One minute past, and Lethe-wards had sunk.
'Tis not through envy of thy happy lot,
  But being too happy in thine happiness –
    That thou, light-winged Dryad of the trees,
      In some melodious plot
Of beechen green, and shadows numberless,
    Singest of summer in full-throated ease.

Oh, for a draught of vintage that hath been
  Cooled a long age in the deep-delvèd earth,
Tasting of Flora and the country green,
  Dance, and Provençal song, and sunburnt mirth!
Oh, for a beaker full of the warm South,
  Full of the true, the blushful Hippocrene,
    With beaded bubbles winking at the brim,
      And purple-stained mouth,
  That I might drink, and leave the world unseen,
    And with thee fade away into the forest dim –

Fade far away, dissolve, and quite forget
  What thou among the leaves hast never known,
The weariness, the fever, and the fret
  Here, where men sit and hear each other groan;
Where palsy shakes a few, sad, last gray hairs,
  Where youth grows pale, and spectre-thin, and dies;
    Where but to think is to be full of sorrow
      And leaden-eyed despairs;
Where Beauty cannot keep her lustrous eyes,
  Or new Love pine at them beyond to-morrow.

[17]

Away! away! For I will fly to thee,
  Not charioted by Bacchus and his pards,
But on the viewless wings of Poesy,
  Though the dull brain perplexes and retards.
Already with thee! Tender is the night,
  And haply the Queen-Moon is on her throne,
    Clustered around by all her starry fays;
      But here there is no light,
  Save what from heaven is with the breezes blown
    Through verdurous glooms and winding mossy ways.

I cannot see what flowers are at my feet,
  Nor what soft incense hangs upon the boughs,
But, in embalmèd darkness, guess each sweet
  Wherewith the seasonable month endows
The grass, the thicket, and the fruit-tree wild –
  White hawthorn, and the pastoral eglantine;
    Fast-fading violets covered up in leaves;
      And mid-May's eldest child,
  The coming musk-rose, full of dewy wine,
    The murmurous haunt of flies on summer eves.

Darkling, I listen; and, for many a time
  I have been half in love with easeful Death,
Called him soft names in many a musèd rhyme,
  To take into the air my quiet breath;
Now more than ever seems it rich to die,
  To cease upon the midnight with no pain,
    While thou art pouring forth thy soul abroad
      In such an ecstasy.
  Still wouldst thou sing, and I have ears in vain –
    To thy high requiem become a sod.

Thou wast not born for death, immortal bird!
  No hungry generations tread thee down;
The voice I hear this passing night was heard
  In ancient days by emperor and clown:
Perhaps the self-same song that found a path
  Through the sad heart of Ruth, when, sick for home,
    She stood in tears amid the alien corn;
      The same that oft-times hath
  Charmed magic casements, opening on the foam
    Of perilous seas in fairy lands forlorn.

Forlorn! The very word is like a bell
  To toll me back from thee to my sole self!
Adieu! The fancy cannot cheat so well
  As she is famed to do, deceiving elf.
Adieu! Adieu! Thy plaintive anthem fades
    Past the near meadows, over the still stream,
      Up the hill-side; and now 'tis buried deep
        In the next valley-glades:
    Was it a vision, or a waking dream?
     Fled is that music . . . Do I wake or sleep?

JOHN KEATS

The Love Song of
J. Alfred Prufrock

LET us go then, you and I,
When the evening is spread out against the sky
Like a patient etherised upon a table;
Let us go, through certain half-deserted streets,
The muttering retreats
Of restless nights in one-night cheap hotels
And sawdust restaurants with oyster-shells:
Streets that follow like a tedious argument
Of insidious intent
To lead you to an overwhelming question . . .
Oh, do not ask, 'What is it?'
Let us go and make our visit.

In the room the women come and go
Talking of Michelangelo.

The yellow fog that rubs its back upon the window-panes,
The yellow smoke that rubs its muzzle on the window-panes,
Licked its tongue into the corners of the evening,
Lingered upon the pools that stand in drains,
Let fall upon its back the soot that falls from chimneys,
Slipped by the terrace, made a sudden leap,
And seeing that it was a soft October night,
Curled once about the house, and fell asleep.

And indeed there will be time
For the yellow smoke that slides along the street
Rubbing its back upon the window-panes;
There will be time, there will be time
To prepare a face to meet the faces that you meet;
There will be time to murder and create,
And time for all the works and days of hands
That lift and drop a question on your plate;
Time for you and time for me,
And time yet for a hundred indecisions,
And for a hundred visions and revisions,
Before the taking of a toast and tea.

In the room the women come and go
Talking of Michelangelo.

And indeed there will be time
To wonder, 'Do I dare?' and, 'Do I dare?'
Time to turn back and descend the stair,
With a bald spot in the middle of my hair
(They will say: 'How his hair is growing thin!')
My morning coat, my collar mounting firmly to the chin,
My necktie rich and modest, but asserted by a simple pin –
(They will say: 'But how his arms and legs are thin!')
Do I dare
Disturb the universe?
In a minute there is time
For decisions and revisions which a minute will reverse.

For I have known them all already, known them all –
Have known the evenings, mornings, afternoons,
I have measured out my life with coffee spoons;
I know the voices dying with a dying fall
Beneath the music from a farther room.
    So how should I presume?

And I have known the eyes already, known them all –
The eyes that fix you in a formulated phrase,
And when I am formulated, sprawling on a pin,
When I am pinned and wriggling on the wall,
Then how should I begin
To spit out all the butt-ends of my days and ways?
    And how should I presume?

And I have known the arms already, known them all –
Arms that are braceleted and white and bare
(But in the lamplight, downed with light brown hair!)
Is it perfume from a dress
That makes me so digress?
Arms that lie along a table, or wrap about a shawl.
    And should I then presume?
    And how should I begin?

         *   *   *

Shall I say, I have gone at dusk through narrow streets
And watched the smoke that rises from the pipes
Of lonely men in shirt-sleeves, leaning out of windows? . . .

    I should have been a pair of ragged claws
Scuttling across the floors of silent seas.

         *   *   *

    And in the afternoon, the evening, sleeps so peacefully!
Smoothed by long fingers,
Asleep . . . tired . . . or it malingers,
Stretched on the floor, here beside you and me.
Should I, after tea and cakes and ices,
Have the strength to force the moment to its crisis?
But though I have wept and fasted, wept and prayed,
Though I have seen my head (grown slightly bald)
    brought in upon a platter,
I am no prophet – and here's no great matter;
I have seen the moment of my greatness flicker,
And I have seen the eternal Footman hold my coat, and snicker,
And in short, I was afraid.

    And would it have been worth it, after all,
After the cups, the marmalade, the tea,
Among the porcelain, among some talk of you and me,
Would it have been worth while,
To have bitten off the matter with a smile,
To have squeezed the universe into a ball
To roll it toward some overwhelming question,
To say: 'I am Lazarus, come from the dead,
Come back to tell you all, I shall tell you all' –
If one, settling a pillow by her head,

Should say: 'That is not what I meant at all.
That is not it, at all.'

And would it have been worth it, after all,
Would it have been worth while,
After the sunsets and the dooryards and the sprinkled streets,
After the novels, after the teacups, after the skirts that trail along the
      floor –
And this, and so much more –
It is impossible to say just what I mean!
But as if a magic lantern threw the nerves in patterns on a screen:
Would it have been worth while
If one, settling a pillow or throwing off a shawl,
And turning toward the window, should say:
    'That is not it at all,
    That is not what I meant, at all.'

               *   *   *

No! I am not Prince Hamlet, nor was meant to be;
Am an attendant lord, one that will do
To swell a progress, start a scene or two,
Advise the prince; no doubt, an easy tool,
Deferential, glad to be of use,
Politic, cautious, and meticulous;
Full of high sentence, but a bit obtuse;
At times, indeed, almost ridiculous –
Almost, at times, the Fool.

    I grow old . . . I grow old . . .
I shall wear the bottoms of my trousers rolled.

    Shall I part my hair behind? Do I dare to eat a peach?
I shall wear white flannel trousers, and walk upon the beach.
I have heard the mermaids singing, each to each.

I do not think that they will sing to me.

I have seen them riding seaward on the waves
Combing the white hair of the waves blown back
When the wind blows the water white and black.

We have lingered in the chambers of the sea
By sea-girls wreathed in seaweed red and brown
Till human voices wake us, and we drown.

                                    T. S. Eliot

Sonnet 18

SHALL I compare thee to a summer's day?
Thou art more lovely and more temperate.
Rough winds do shake the darling buds of May,
And summer's lease hath all too short a date.
Sometime too hot the eye of heaven shines,
And often is his gold complexion dimmed,
And every fair from fair sometimes declines,
By chance or nature's changing course untrimmed;
But thy eternal summer shall not fade,
Nor lose possession of that fair thou ow'st,
Nor shall Death brag thou wander'st in his shade,
When in eternal lines to time thou grow'st.
    So long as men can breathe or eyes can see,
    So long lives this, and this gives life to thee.

WILLIAM SHAKESPEARE

Dover Beach

THE sea is calm tonight.
The tide is full, the moon lies fair
Upon the straits; – on the French coast the light
Gleams and is gone; the cliffs of England stand,
Glimmering and vast, out in the tranquil bay.
Come to the window, sweet is the night-air!
Only, from the long line of spray
Where the sea meets the moon-blanch'd land,
Listen! you hear the grating roar
Of pebbles which the waves draw back, and fling,
At their return, up the high strand,
Begin, and cease, and then again begin,
With tremulous cadence slow, and bring
The eternal note of sadness in.
Sophocles long ago
Heard it on the Ægæan, and it brought
Into his mind the turbid ebb and flow
Of human misery; we
Find also in the sound a thought,
Hearing it by this distant northern sea.

The Sea of Faith
Was once, too, at the full, and round earth's shore
Lay like the folds of a bright girdle furl'd.
But now I only hear
Its melancholy, long, withdrawing roar,
Retreating, to the breath
Of the night-wind, down the vast edges drear
And naked shingles of the world.

Ah, love, let us be true
To one another! for the world, which seems
To lie before us like a land of dreams,
So various, so beautiful, so new,
Hath really neither joy, nor love, nor light,
Nor certitude, nor peace, nor help for pain;
And we are here as on a darkling plain
Swept with confused alarms of struggle and flight,
Where ignorant armies clash by night.

MATTHEW ARNOLD

To Autumn

SEASON of mists and mellow fruitfulness,
   Close bosom friend of the maturing sun,
Conspiring with him how to load and bless
   With fruit the vines that round the thatch-eves run:
To bend with apples the mossed cottage-trees,
   And fill all fruit with ripeness to the core;
      To swell the gourd, and plump the hazel shells
   With a sweet kernel; to set budding more,
And still more, later flowers for the bees,
Until they think warm days will never cease,
      For summer has o'er-brimmed their clammy cells.

Who hath not seen thee oft amid thy store?
   Sometimes whoever seeks abroad may find
Thee sitting careless on a granary floor,
   Thy hair soft-lifted by the winnowing wind;
Or on a half-reaped furrow sound asleep,
   Drowsed with the fume of poppies, while thy hook
      Spares the next swath and all its twinèd flowers;
And sometimes like a gleaner thou dost keep
   Steady thy laden head across a brook;
   Or by a cyder-press, with patient look,
      Thou watchest the last oozings hours by hours.

Where are the songs of spring? Aye, where are they?
   Think not of them, thou hast thy music too –
While barrèd clouds bloom the soft-dying day,
   And touch the stubble-plains with rosy hue.
Then in a wailful choir the small gnats mourn
   Among the river sallows, borne aloft
      Or sinking as the light wind lives or dies;
And full-grown lambs loud bleat from hilly bourn;
   Hedge-crickets sing; and now with treble soft
   The red-breast whistles from a garden-croft;
      And gathering swallows twitter in the skies.

JOHN KEATS

from *The Rime of the Ancient Mariner*

೨೦೧೮೦೧೮೦೧೮೦೧೮೦

Part I

An ancient Mariner
meeteth three
Gallants bidden to a
wedding-feast, and
detaineth one.

It is an ancient Mariner,
And he stoppeth one of three.
'By thy long grey beard and glittering eye,
Now wherefore stopp'st thou me?

The Bridegroom's doors are opened wide,
And I am next of kin;
The guests are met, the feast is set:
May'st hear the merry din.'

He holds him with his skinny hand,
'There was a ship,' quoth he.
'Hold off! unhand me, grey-beard loon!'
Eftsoons his hand dropt he.

The Wedding-Guest
is spellbound by the
eye of the old
seafaring man, and
constrained to hear
his tale.

He holds him with his glittering eye –
The Wedding-Guest stood still,
And listens like a three years' child:
The Mariner hath his will.

The Wedding-Guest sat on a stone:
He cannot choose but hear;
And thus spake on that ancient man,
The bright-eyed Mariner.

'The ship was cheered, the harbour cleared,
Merrily did we drop
Below the kirk, below the hill,
Below the lighthouse top.

The Mariner tells
how the ship sailed
southward with a
good wind and fair
weather, till it
reached the Line.

The Sun came up upon the left,
Out of the sea came he!
And he shone bright, and on the right
Went down into the sea.

Higher and higher every day,
Till over the mast at noon –'
The Wedding-Guest here beat his breast,
For he heard the loud bassoon.

The Wedding-Guest heareth the bridal music; but the Mariner continueth his tale.

The bride hath paced into the hall,
Red as a rose is she;
Nodding their heads before her goes
The merry minstrelsy.

The Wedding-Guest he beat his breast,
Yet he cannot choose but hear;
And thus spake on that ancient man,
The bright-eyed Mariner.

The ship driven by a storm toward the south pole.

'And now the Storm-blast came, and he
Was tyrannous and strong:
He struck with his o'ertaking wings,
And chased us south along.

With sloping masts and dipping prow,
As who pursued with yell and blow
Still treads the shadow of his foe,
And forward bends his head,
The ship drove fast, loud roared the blast,
And southward aye we fled.

And now there came both mist and snow,
And it grew wondrous cold:
And ice, mast-high, came floating by,
As green as emerald.

The land of ice, and of fearful sounds where no living thing was to be seen.

And through the drifts the snowy clifts
Did send a dismal sheen:
Nor shapes of men nor beasts we ken –
The ice was all between.

The ice was here, the ice was there,
The ice was all around:
It cracked and growled, and roared and howled,
Like noises in a swound!

Till a great sea-bird, called the Albatross, came through the snow-fog, and was received with great joy and hospitality.

At length did cross an Albatross,
Thorough the fog it came;
As if it had been a Christian soul,
We hailed it in God's name.

It ate the food it ne'er had eat,
And round and round it flew.
The ice did split with a thunder-fit;
The helmsman steered us through!

And lo! the Albatross proveth a bird of good omen, and followeth the ship as it returned northward through fog and floating ice.

And a good south wind sprung up behind;
The Albatross did follow,
And every day, for food or play,
Came to the Mariners' hollo!

In mist or cloud, on mast or shroud,
It perched for vespers nine;
Whiles all the night, through fog-smoke white,
Glimmered the white Moon-shine.'

The ancient Mariner inhospitably killeth the pious bird of good omen.

'God save thee, ancient Mariner!
From the fiends, that plague thee thus! –
Why look'st thou so?' – With my cross-bow
I shot the Albatross.

Part II

The Sun now rose upon the right:
Out of the sea came he,
Still hid in mist, and on the left
Went down into the sea.

And the good south wind still blew behind,
But no sweet bird did follow,
Nor any day for food or play
Came to the mariner's hollo!

His shipmates cry out against the ancient Mariner, for killing the bird of good luck.

And I had done a hellish thing,
And it would work 'em woe:
For all averred, I had killed the bird
That made the breeze to blow.
Ah wretch! said they, the bird to slay,
That made the breeze to blow!

But when the fog cleared off, they justify the same, and thus make themselves accomplices in the crime.

Nor dim nor red, like God's own head,
The glorious Sun uprist:
Then all averred, I had killed the bird
That brought the fog and mist.
'Twas right, said they, such birds to slay,
That bring the fog and mist.

The fair breeze continues; the ship enters the Pacific Ocean, and sails northward, even till it reaches the Line.

The fair breeze blew, the white foam flew,
The furrow followed free;
We were the first that ever burst
Into that silent sea.

Down dropt the breeze, the sails dropt down,
'Twas sad as sad could be;
And we did speak only to break
The silence of the sea!

All in a hot and copper sky,
The bloody Sun, at noon,
Right up above the mast did stand,
No bigger than the Moon.

Day after day, day after day,
We stuck, nor breath nor motion;
As idle as a painted ship
Upon a painted ocean.

And the Albatross
begins to be
avenged.

Water, water, every where,
And all the boards did shrink;
Water, water, every where,
Nor any drop to drink.

The very deep did rot: O Christ!
That ever this should be!
Yea, slimy things did crawl with legs
Upon the slimy sea.

A Spirit had
followed them; one
of the invisible
inhabitants of this
planet, neither
departed souls nor
angels; concerning
whom the learned
Jew, Josephus, and
the Platonic
Constantinopolitan,
Michael Psellus,
may be consulted.
They are very
numerous, and there
is no climate or
element without one
or more.

About, about, in reel and rout
The death-fires danced at night;
The water, like a witch's oils,
Burnt green, and blue and white.

And some in dreams assuréd were
Of the Spirit that plagued us so;
Nine fathom deep he had followed us
From the land of mist and snow.

The shipmates, in
their sore distress,
would fain throw
the whole guilt on
the ancient Mariner:
in sign whereof they
hang the dead sea-
bird round his neck.

And every tongue, through utter drought,
Was withered at the root;
We could not speak, no more than if
We had been choked with soot.

Ah! well a-day! what evil looks
Had I from old and young!
Instead of the cross, the Albatross
About my neck was hung.

[31]

Part III

There passed a weary time. Each throat
Was parched, and glazed each eye.
A weary time! a weary time!
How glazed each weary eye,
When looking westward, I beheld
A something in the sky.

The ancient Mariner beholdeth a sign in the element afar off.

At first it seemed a little speck,
And then it seemed a mist;
It moved and moved, and took at last
A certain shape, I wist.

A speck, a mist, a shape, I wist!
And still it neared and neared:
As if it dodged a water-sprite,
It plunged and tacked and veered.

At its nearer approach, it seemeth to him to be a ship; and at a dear ransom he freeth his speech from the bonds of thirst.

With throats unslaked, with black lips baked,
We could nor laugh nor wail;
Through utter drought all dumb we stood!
I bit my arm, I sucked the blood,
And cried, A sail! a sail!

With throats unslaked, with black lips baked,
Agape they heard me call:

A flash of joy;

Gramercy! they for joy did grin,
And all at once their breath drew in,
As they were drinking all.

And horror follows. For can it be a ship that comes onward without wind or tide?

See! see! (I cried) she tacks no more!
Hither to work us weal;
Without a breeze, without a tide,
She steadies with upright keel!

The western wave was all a-flame.
The day was well nigh done!
Almost upon the western wave
Rested the broad bright Sun;
When that strange shape drove suddenly
Betwixt us and the Sun.

It seemeth him but the skeleton of a ship.

And straight the Sun was flecked with bars,
(Heaven's Mother send us grace!)

As if through a dungeon-grate he peered
With broad and burning face.

Alas! (thought I, and my heart beat loud)
How fast she nears and nears!

And its ribs are seen as bars on the face of the setting Sun.

Are those her sails that glance in the Sun,
Like restless gossameres?

The Spectre-Woman and her Death-mate, and no other on board the skeleton ship.

Are those her ribs through which the Sun
Did peer, as through a grate?
And is that Woman all her crew?
Is that a Death? and are there two?
Is Death that woman's mate?

Like vessel, like crew!

Death and Life-in-Death have diced for the ship's crew, and she (the latter) winneth the ancient Mariner.

Her lips were red, her looks were free,
Her locks were yellow as gold:
Her skin was as white as leprosy,
The Night-mare Life-in-Death was she,
Who thicks man's blood with cold.

The naked hulk alongside came,
And the twain were casting dice;
'The game is done! I've won! I've won!'
Quoth she, and whistles thrice.

No twilight within the courts of the Sun.

The Sun's rim dips; the stars rush out:
At one stride comes the dark;
With far-heard whisper, o'er the sea,
Off shot the spectre-bark.

At the rising of the Moon,

We listened and looked sideways up!
Fear at my heart, as at a cup,
My life-blood seemed to sip!
The stars were dim, and thick the night,
The steersman's face by his lamp gleamed white;
From the sails the dew did drip –
Till clomb above the eastern bar
The hornéd Moon, with one bright star
Within the nether tip.

One after another,

One after one, by the star-dogged Moon,
Too quick for groan or sigh,
Each turned his face with a ghastly pang,
And cursed me with his eye.

[33]

His shipmates drop
down dead.

Four times fifty living men,
(And I heard nor sigh nor groan)
With heavy thump, a lifeless lump,
They dropped down one by one.

But Life-in-Death
begins her work on
the ancient Mariner.

The souls did from their bodies fly,
They fled to bliss or woe!
And every soul, it passed me by,
Like the whizz of my cross-bow!

SAMUEL TAYLOR COLERIDGE

Sonnet 29

WHEN, in disgrace with Fortune and men's eyes,
I all alone beweep my outcast state,
And trouble deaf heaven with my bootless cries,
And look upon myself and curse my fate,
Wishing me like to one more rich in hope,
Featured like him, like him with friends possessed,
Desiring this man's art and that man's scope,
With what I most enjoy contented least;
Yet in these thoughts myself almost despising
Haply I think on thee, and then my state,
Like to the lark at break of day arising
From sullen earth, sings hymns at heaven's gate:
 For thy sweet love remember'd such wealth brings
 That then I scorn to change my state with kings.

WILLIAM SHAKESPEARE

'So, we'll go no more a roving'

So, we'll go no more a roving
   So late into the night,
Though the heart be still as loving,
   And the moon be still as bright.

For the sword outwears its sheath,
   And the soul wears out the breast,
And the heart must pause to breathe,
   And love itself have rest.

Though the night was made for loving,
   And the day returns too soon,
Yet we'll go no more a roving
   By the light of the moon.

LORD BYRON

from *Ode: Intimations of Immortality*

THERE was a time when meadow, grove, and stream,
The earth, and every common sight,
    To me did seem
  Apparelled in celestial light,
The glory and the freshness of a dream.
It is now as it hath been of yore;
  Turn wheresoe'er I may,
    By night or day,
The things which I have seen I now can see no more.

    The Rainbow comes and goes,
    And lovely is the Rose,
    The Moon doth with delight
Look round her when the heavens are bare,
    Waters on a starry night
    And beautiful and fair;
  The sunshine is a glorious birth;
  But yet I know, where'er I go,
That there hath past away a glory from the earth.

Now, while the birds thus sing a joyous song,
  And while the young lambs bound
    As to the tabor's sound,
To me alone there came a thought of grief:
A timely utterance gave that thought relief,
    And I again am strong:
The cataracts blow their trumpets from the steep;
No more shall grief of mine the season wrong:
I hear the Echoes through the mountains throng,
The Winds come to me from the fields of sleep,
And all the earth is gay.
  Land and sea
Give themselves up to jollity,
  And with the heart of May
Doth every Beast keep holiday.
  Thou Child of Joy,
Shout round me, let me hear thy shouts, thou happy shepherd-boy!

WILLIAM WORDSWORTH

[37]

The Whitsun Weddings

THAT Whitsun, I was late getting away:
   Not till about
One-twenty on the sunlit Saturday
Did my three-quarters-empty train pull out,
All windows down, all cushions hot, all sense
Of being in a hurry gone. We ran
Behind the backs of houses, crossed a street
Of blinding windscreens, smelt the fish-dock; thence
The river's level drifting breadth began,
Where sky and Lincolnshire and water meet.

All afternoon, through the tall heat that slept
   For miles inland,
A slow and stopping curve southwards we kept.
Wide farms went by, short-shadowed cattle, and
Canals with floatings of industrial froth;
A hothouse flashed uniquely: hedges dipped
And rose: and now and then a smell of grass
Displaced the reek of buttoned carriage-cloth
Until the next town, new and nondescript,
Approached with acres of dismantled cars.

At first, I didn't notice what a noise
   The weddings made
Each station that we stopped at: sun destroys
The interest of what's happening in the shade,
And down the long cool platforms whoops and skirls
I took for porters larking with the mails,
And went on reading. Once we started, though,
We passed them, grinning and pomaded, girls
In parodies of fashion, heels and veils,
All posed irresolutely, watching us go,

As if out on the end of an event
    Waving goodbye
To something that survived it. Struck, I leant
More promptly out next time, more curiously,
And saw it all again in different terms:
The fathers with broad belts under their suits
And seamy foreheads; mothers loud and fat;
An uncle shouting smut; and then the perms,
The nylon gloves and jewellery-substitutes,
The lemons, mauves, and olive-ochres that

Marked off the girls unreally from the rest.
    Yes, from cafés
And banquet-halls up yards, and bunting-dressed
Coach-party annexes, the wedding-days
Were coming to an end. All down the line
Fresh couples climbed aboard: the rest stood round;
The last confetti and advice were thrown,
And, as we moved, each face seemed to define
Just what it saw departing: children frowned
At something dull; fathers had never known

Success so huge and wholly farcical;
    The women shared
The secret like a happy funeral;
While girls, gripping their handbags tighter, stared
At a religious wounding. Free at last,
And loaded with the sum of all they saw,
We hurried towards London, shuffling gouts of steam.
Now fields were building-plots, and poplars cast
Long shadows over major roads, and for
Some fifty minutes, that in time would seem

Just long enough to settle hats and say
    I nearly died,
A dozen marriages got under way.
They watched the landscape, sitting side by side
– An Odeon went past, a cooling tower,
And someone running up to bowl – and none
Thought of the others they would never meet
Or how their lives would all contain this hour.
I thought of London spread out in the sun,
Its postal districts packed like squares of wheat:

There we were aimed. And as we raced across
   Bright knots of rail
Past standing Pullmans, walls of blackened moss
Came close, and it was nearly done, this frail
Travelling coincidence; and what it held
Stood ready to be loosed with all the power
That being changed can give. We slowed again,
And as the tightened brakes took hold, there swelled
A sense of falling, like an arrow-shower
Sent out of sight, somewhere becoming rain.

PHILIP LARKIN

Anthem for Doomed Youth

WHAT passing-bells for these who die as cattle?
  Only the monstrous anger of the guns.
  Only the stuttering rifles' rapid rattle
Can patter out their hasty orisons.
No mockeries for them from prayers or bells,
  Nor any voice of mourning save the choirs, –
The shrill, demented choirs of wailing shells;
  And bugles calling for them from sad shires.

What candles may be held to speed them all?
  Not in the hands of boys, but in their eyes
Shall shine the holy glimmers of good-byes.
  The pallor of girls' brows shall be their pall;
Their flowers the tenderness of silent minds,
And each slow dusk a drawing-down of blinds.

WILFRED OWEN

Sonnet 60

Like as the waves make towards the pebbled shore,
So do our minutes hasten to their end;
Each changing place with that which goes before
In sequent toil all forwards do contend.
Nativity, once in the main of light,
Crawls to maturity, wherewith being crowned,
Crookèd eclipses 'gainst his glory fight,
And Time that gave doth now his gift confound.
Time doth transfix the flourish set on youth,
And delves the parallels in beauty's brow,
Feeds on the rarities of nature's truth;
And nothing stands but for his scythe to mow.
    And yet to times in hope my verse shall stand,
    Praising thy worth, despite his cruel hand.

WILLIAM SHAKESPEARE

Tintern Abbey

Lines composed a few miles above Tintern Abbey, on
revisiting the banks of the Wye during a tour. July 13, 1798

FIVE years have past; five summers, with the length
Of five long winters! and again I hear
These waters, rolling from their mountain-springs
With a sweet inland murmur. – Once again
Do I behold these steep and lofty cliffs,
That on a wild secluded scene impress
Thoughts of more deep seclusion; and connect
The landscape with the quiet of the sky.
The day is come when I again repose
Here, under this dark sycamore, and view
These plots of cottage-ground, these orchard-tufts,
Which at this season, with their unripe fruits,
Are clad in one green hue, and lose themselves
Among the woods and copses, nor disturb
The wild green landscape. Once again I see
These hedge-rows, hardly hedge-rows, little lines
Of sportive wood run wild: these pastoral farms,
Green to the very door; and wreaths of smoke
Sent up, in silence, from among the trees!
With some uncertain notice, as might seem
Of vagrant dwellers in the houseless woods,
Or of some Hermit's cave, where by his fire
The Hermit sits alone.

     These beauteous forms,
Through a long absence, have not been to me
As is a landscape to a blind man's eye:
But oft, in lonely rooms, and 'mid the din
Of towns and cities, I have owed to them,
In hours of weariness, sensations sweet,

Felt in the blood, and felt along the heart;
And passing even into my purer mind,
With tranquil restoration: – feelings too
Of unremembered pleasure: such, perhaps,
As have no slight or trivial influence
On that best portion of a good man's life,
His little, nameless, unremembered acts
Of kindness and of love. Nor less, I trust,
To them I may have owed another gift,
Of aspect more sublime; that blessed mood,
In which the burthen of the mystery,
In which the heavy and the weary weight
Of all this unintelligible world,
Is lightened: – that serene and blessed mood,
In which the affections gently lead us on, –
Until, the breath of this corporeal frame
And even the motion of our human blood
Almost suspended, we are laid asleep
In body, and become a living soul:
While with an eye made quiet by the power
Of harmony, and the deep power of joy,
We see into the life of things.

                                    If this
Be but a vain belief, yet, oh! how oft –
In darkness and amid the many shapes
Of joyless daylight; when the fretful stir
Unprofitable, and the fever of the world,
Have hung upon the beatings of my heart –
How oft, in spirit, have I turned to thee,
O sylvan Wye! Thou wanderer thro' the woods,
How often has my spirit turned to thee!

      And now, with gleams of half-extinguished thought,
With many recognitions dim and faint,
And somewhat of a sad perplexity,
The picture of the mind revives again:
While here I stand, not only with the sense
Of present pleasure, but with pleasing thoughts
That in this moment there is life and food
For future years. And so I dare to hope,

Though changed, no doubt, from what I was when first
I came among these hills; when like a roe
I bounded o'er the mountains, by the sides
Of the deep rivers, and the lonely streams,
Wherever nature led: more like a man
Flying from something that he dreads, than one
Who sought the thing he loved. For nature then
(The coarser pleasures of my boyish days,
And their glad animal movements all gone by)
To me was all in all. — I cannot paint
What then I was. The sounding cataract
Haunted me like a passion: the tall rock,
The mountain, and the deep and gloomy wood,
Their colours and their forms, were then to me
An appetite; a feeling and a love,
That had no need of a remoter charm,
By thought supplied, nor any interest
Unborrowed from the eye. — That time is past,
And all its aching joys are now no more,
And all its dizzy raptures. Not for this
Faint I, nor mourn nor murmur; other gifts
Have followed; for such loss, I would believe,
Abundant recompense. For I have learned
To look on nature, not as in the hour
Of thoughtless youth; but hearing oftentimes
The still, sad music of humanity,
Nor harsh nor grating, though of ample power
To chasten and subdue. And I have felt
A presence that disturbs me with the joy
Of elevated thoughts; a sense sublime
Of something far more deeply interfused,
Whose dwelling is the light of setting suns,
And the round ocean and the living air,
And the blue sky, and in the mind of man:
A motion and a spirit, that impels
All thinking things, all objects of all thought,
And rolls through all things. Therefore am I still
A lover of the meadows and the woods,
And mountains; and of all that we behold
From this green earth; of all the mighty world
Of eye, and ear, — both what they half create,
And what perceive; well pleased to recognise

In nature and the language of the sense,
The anchor of my purest thoughts, the nurse,
The guide, the guardian of my heart, and soul
Of all my moral being.

                              Nor perchance,
If I were not thus taught, should I the more
Suffer my genial spirits to decay:
For thou art with me here upon the banks
Of this fair river; thou my dearest Friend,
My dear, dear Friend; and in thy voice I catch
The language of my former heart, and read
My former pleasures in the shooting lights
Of thy wild eyes. Oh! yet a little while
May I behold in thee what I was once,
My dear, dear Sister! and this prayer I make,
Knowing that Nature never did betray
The heart that loved her; 'tis her privilege,
Through all the years of this our life, to lead
From joy to joy: for she can so inform
The mind that is within us, so impress
With quietness and beauty, and so feed
With lofty thoughts, that neither evil tongues,
Rash judgments, nor the sneers of selfish men,
Nor greetings where no kindness is, nor all
The dreary intercourse of daily life,
Shall e'er prevail against us, or disturb
Our cheerful faith, that all which we behold
Is full of blessings. Therefore let the moon
Shine on thee in thy solitary walk;
And let the misty mountain-winds be free
To blow against thee: and, in after years,
When these wild ecstasies shall be matured
Into a sober pleasure; when thy mind
Shall be a mansion for all lovely forms,
Thy memory be as a dwelling-place
For all sweet sounds and harmonies; oh! then,
If solitude, or fear, or pain, or grief,
Should be thy portion, with what healing thoughts
Of tender joy wilt thou remember me,
And these my exhortations! Nor, perchance –
If I should be where I no more can hear

Thy voice, nor catch from thy wild eyes these gleams
Of past existence – wilt thou then forget
That on the banks of this delightful stream
We stood together; and that I, so long
A worshipper of Nature, hither came
Unwearied in that service: rather say
With warmer love – oh! with far deeper zeal
Of holier love. Nor wilt thou then forget,
That after many wanderings, many years
Of absence, these steep woods and lofty cliffs,
And this green pastoral landscape, were to me
More dear, both for themselves and for thy sake!

WILLIAM WORDSWORTH

'How do I love thee?'

How do I love thee? Let me count the ways.
I love thee to the depth and breadth and height
My soul can reach, when feeling out of sight
For the ends of Being and ideal Grace.
I love thee to the level of every day's
Most quiet need, by sun and candlelight.
I love thee freely, as men strive for Right;
I love thee purely, as they turn from Praise.
I love thee with the passion put to use
In my old griefs, and with my childhood's faith.
I love thee with a love I seemed to lose
With my lost saints, – I love thee with the breath,
Smiles, tears, of all my life! – and, if God choose,
I shall but love thee better after death.

ELIZABETH BARRETT BROWNING
from Sonnets from the Portuguese, xliii

'My love is like a red, red rose'

My love is like a red, red rose
   That's newly sprung in June:
My love is like the melodie
   That's sweetly played in tune.

So fair art thou, my bonny lass,
   So deep in love am I:
And I will love thee still, my dear,
   Till a' the seas gang dry.

Till a' the seas gang dry, my dear,
   And the rocks melt wi' the sun:
And I will love thee still, my dear,
   While the sands o' life shall run.

And fare thee weel, my only love,
   And fare thee weel awhile!
And I will come again, my love,
   Tho' it were ten thousand mile.

ROBERT BURNS

If —

IF you can keep your head when all about you
  Are losing theirs and blaming it on you;
If you can trust yourself when all men doubt you,
  But make allowance for their doubting too;
If you can wait and not be tired by waiting,
  Or, being lied about, don't deal in lies,
Or, being hated, don't give way to hating,
  And yet don't look too good, nor talk too wise;

If you can dream – and not make dreams your master;
  If you can think – and not make thoughts your aim;
If you can meet with triumph and disaster
  And treat those two impostors just the same;
If you can bear to hear the truth you've spoken
  Twisted by knaves to make a trap for fools,
Or watch the things you gave your life to broken,
  And stoop and build 'em up with wornout tools;

If you can make one heap of all your winnings
  And risk it on one turn of pitch-and-toss,
And lose, and start again at your beginnings
  And never breathe a word about your loss;
If you can force your heart and nerve and sinew
  To serve your turn long after they are gone,
And so hold on when there is nothing in you
  Except the Will which says to them: 'Hold on';

If you can talk with crowds and keep your virtue,
  Or walk with kings – nor lose the common touch;
If neither foes nor loving friends can hurt you;
  If all men count with you, but none too much;
If you can fill the unforgiving minute
  With sixty seconds' worth of distance run –
Yours is the Earth and everything that's in it,
  And – which is more – you'll be a Man, my son!

RUDYARD KIPLING

[50]

from *The Ballad of Reading Gaol*

In Debtors' Yard the stones are hard,
  And the dripping wall is high,
So it was there he took his air
  Beneath the leaden sky,
And by each side a warder walked,
  For fear the man might die.

Or else he sat with those who watched
  His anguish night and day;
Who watched him when he rose to weep,
  And when he crouched to pray;
Who watched him lest himself should rob
  Their scaffold of its prey.

The Governor was strong upon
  The Regulations Act:
The Doctor said that Death was but
  A scientific fact:
And twice a day the Chaplain called,
  And left a little tract.

And twice a day he smoked his pipe,
  And drank his quart of beer:
His soul was resolute, and held
  No hiding-place for fear;
He often said that he was glad
  The hangman's day was near.

But why he said so strange a thing
  No warder dared to ask:
For he to whom a watcher's doom
  Is given as his task,
Must set a lock upon his lips
  And make his face a mask.

Or else he might be moved, and try
  To comfort or console:
And what should Human Pity do
  Pent up in Murderer's Hole?
What word of grace in such a place
  Could help a brother's soul?

[51]

With slouch and swing around the ring
  We trod the Fools' Parade!
We did not care: we knew we were
  The Devil's Own Brigade:
And shaven head and feet of lead
  Make a merry masquerade.

We tore the tarry rope to shreds
  With blunt and bleeding nails;
We rubbed the doors, and scrubbed the floors,
  And cleaned the shining rails:
And, rank by rank, we soaped the plank,
  And clattered with the pails.

We sewed the sacks, we broke the stones,
  We turned the dusty drill:
We banged the tins, and bawled the hymns,
  And sweated on the mill:
But in the heart of every man
  Terror was lying still.

So still it lay that every day
  Crawled like a weed–clogged wave:
And we forgot the bitter lot
  That waits for fool and knave,
Till once, as we tramped in from work,
  We passed an open grave.

With yawning mouth the yellow hole
  Gaped for a living thing;
The very mud cried out for blood
  To the thirsty asphalt ring;
And we knew that ere one dawn grew fair
  Some prisoner had to swing.

Right in we went, with soul intent
  On Death and Dread and Doom:
The hangman, with his little bag,
  Went shuffling through the gloom:
And I trembled as I groped my way
  Into my numbered tomb.

*   *   *

That night the empty corridors
  Were full of forms of Fear,
And up and down the iron town
  Stole feet we could not hear,
And through the bars that hide the stars
  White faces seemed to peer.

He lay as one who lies and dreams
  In a pleasant meadow-land,
The watchers watched him as he slept,
  And could not understand
How one could sleep so sweet a sleep
  With a hangman close at hand.

But there is no sleep when men must weep
  Who never yet have wept:
So we – the fool, the fraud, the knave –
  That endless vigil kept,
And through each brain on hands of pain
  Another's terror crept.

Alas! it is a fearful thing
  To feel another's guilt!
For right within, the Sword of Sin
  Pierced to its poisoned hilt,
And as molten lead were the tears we shed
  For the blood we had not spilt.

The warders with their shoes of felt
  Crept by each padlocked door,
And peeped and saw, with eyes of awe,
  Grey figures on the floor,
And wondered why men knelt to pray
  Who never prayed before.

All through the night we knelt and prayed,
  Mad mourners of a corse;
The troubled plumes of midnight shook
  Like the plumes upon a hearse;
The bitter wine upon a sponge
  Was the savour of Remorse.

*   *   *

[53]

The grey cock crew, the red cock crew,
  But never came the day:
And crooked shapes of Terror crouched,
  In the corners where we lay:
And each evil sprite that walks by night
  Before us seemed to play.

They glided past, they glided fast,
  Like travellers through a mist:
They mocked the moon in a rigadoon
  Of delicate turn and twist,
And with formal pace and loathsome grace
  The phantoms kept their tryst.

With mop and mow, we saw them go,
  Slim shadows hand in hand:
About, about, in ghostly rout
  They trod a saraband:
And the damned grotesques made arabesques,
  Like the wind upon the sand!

With the pirouettes of marionettes,
  They tripped on pointed tread:
But with flutes of Fear they filled the ear,
  As their grisly masque they led,
And loud they sang, and long they sang,
  For they sang to wake the dead.

'Oho!' they cried, 'The world is wide,
  But fettered limbs go lame!
And once, or twice, to throw the dice
  Is a gentlemanly game,
But he does not win who plays with Sin
  In the secret House of Shame.'

No things of air these antics were,
  That frolicked with such glee:
To men whose lives were held in gyves,
  And whose feet might not go free,
Ah! wounds of Christ! they were living things,
  Most terrible to see.

Around, around, they waltzed and wound;
  Some wheeled in smirking pairs;
With the mincing step of a demirep

Some sidled up the stairs;
  And with subtle sneer, and fawning leer,
    Each helped us at our prayers.

The morning wind began to moan,
  But still the night went on:
Through its giant loom the web of gloom
  Crept till each thread was spun:
And, as we prayed, we grew afraid
  Of the Justice of the Sun.

The moaning wind went wandering round
  The weeping prison-wall:
Till like a wheel of turning steel
  We felt the minutes crawl:
O moaning wind! what had we done
  To have such a seneschal?

At last I saw the shadowed bars,
  Like a lattice wrought in lead,
Move right across the whitewashed wall
  That faced my three-plank bed,
And I knew that somewhere in the world
  God's dreadful dawn was red.

At six o'clock we cleaned our cells,
  At seven all was still,
But the sough and swing of a mighty wing
  The prison seemed to fill,
But the Lord of Death with icy breath
  Had entered in to kill.

He did not pass in purple pomp,
  Nor ride a moon-white steed.
Three yards of cord and a sliding board
  Are all the gallows' need:
So with rope of shame the Herald came
  To do the secret deed.

We were as men who through a fen
  Of filthy darkness grope:
We did not dare to breathe a prayer,
  Or to give our anguish scope:
Something was dead in each of us,
  And what was dead was Hope.

For Man's grim Justice goes its way,
    And will not swerve aside:
It slays the weak, it slays the strong,
    It has a dreadly stride:
With iron heel it slays the strong,
    The monstrous parricide!

We waited for the stroke of eight:
    Each tongue was thick with thirst:
For the stroke of eight is the stroke of Fate
    That makes a man accursed,
And Fate will use a running noose
    For the best man and the worst.

We had no other thing to do,
    Save to wait for the sign to come:
So, like things of stone in a valley lone,
    Quiet we sat and dumb:
But each man's heart beat thick and quick,
    Like a madman on a drum!

With sudden shock the prison-clock
    Smote on the shivering air,
And from all the gaol rose up a wail
    Of impotent despair,
Like the sound that frightened marshes hear
    From some leper in his lair.

And as one sees most fearful things
    In the crystal of a dream,
We saw the greasy hempen rope
    Hooked to the blackened beam,
And heard the prayer the hangman's snare
    Strangled into a scream.

And all the woe that moved him so
    That he gave that bitter cry,
And the wild regrets, and the bloody sweats,
    None knew so well as I:
For he who lives more lives than one
    More deaths than one must die.

OSCAR WILDE

Ozymandias

ɷ

I MET a traveller from an antique land
Who said: Two vast and trunkless legs of stone
Stand in the desert. Near them on the sand,
Half sunk, a shatter'd visage lies, whose frown
And wrinkled lip and sneer of cold command
Tell that its sculptor well those passions read
Which yet survive, stamp'd on these lifeless things,
The hand that mock'd them and the heart that fed;
And on the pedestal these words appear:
'My name is Ozymandias, king of kings:
Look on my works, ye Mighty, and despair!'
Nothing beside remains. Round the decay
Of that colossal wreck, boundless and bare,
The lone and level sands stretch far away.

PERCY BYSSHE SHELLEY

from *A Shropshire Lad*

ᬠ

FROM far, from eve and morning
  And yon twelve-winded sky,
The stuff of life to knit me
  Blew hither: here am I.

Now – for a breath I tarry
  Nor yet disperse apart –
Take my hand quick and tell me,
  What have you in your heart.

Speak now, and I will answer;
  How shall I help you, say:
Ere to the wind's twelve quarters
  I take my endless way.

A. E. HOUSMAN

When You are Old

WHEN you are old and grey and full of sleep,
And nodding by the fire, take down this book,
And slowly read, and dream of the soft look
Your eyes had once, and of their shadows deep;

How many loved your moments of glad grace,
And loved your beauty with love false or true,
But one man loved the pilgrim soul in you,
And loved the sorrows of your changing face;

And bending down beside the glowing bars,
Murmur, a little sadly, how Love fled
And paced upon the mountains overhead
And hid his face amid a crowd of stars.

W. B. YEATS

The Second Coming

TURNING and turning in the widening gyre
The falcon cannot hear the falconer;
Things fall apart; the centre cannot hold;
Mere anarchy is loosed upon the world,
The blood-dimmed tide is loosed, and everywhere
The ceremony of innocence is drowned;
The best lack all conviction, while the worst
Are full of passionate intensity.

Surely some revelation is at hand;
Surely the Second Coming is at hand.
The Second Coming! Hardly are those words out
When a vast image out of *Spiritus Mundi*
Troubles my sight: somewhere in sands of the desert
A shape with lion body and the head of a man,
A gaze blank and pitiless as the sun,
Is moving its slow thighs, while all about it
Reel shadows of the indignant desert birds.
The darkness drops again; but now I know
That twenty centuries of stony sleep
Were vexed to nightmare by a rocking cradle,
And what rough beast, its hour come round at last,
Slouches towards Bethlehem to be born?

W. B. YEATS

The Good-Morrow

I WONDER by my troth, what thou, and I
Did, till we lov'd? were we not wean'd till then?
But suck'd on countrey pleasures, childishly?
Or snorted we i' the seaven sleepers den?
'Twas so; But this, all pleasures fancies bee.
If ever any beauty I did see,
Which I desir'd, and got, 'twas but a dreame of thee.

And now good morrow to our waking soules,
Which watch not one another out of feare;
For love, all love of other sights controules,
And makes one little roome, an every where.
Let sea-discoverers to new worlds have gone,
Let Maps to others, worlds on worlds have showne,
Let us possesse our world, each hath one, and is one.

My face in thine eye, thine in mine appeares,
And true plaine hearts doe in the faces rest,
Where can we finde two better hemispheares
Without sharpe North, without declining West?
What ever dyes, was not mixt equally;
If our two loves be one, or, thou and I
Love so alike, that none doe slacken, none can die.

JOHN DONNE

The Old Vicarage, Grantchester

JUST now the lilac is in bloom,
All before my little room;
And in my flower-beds, I think,
Smile the carnation and the pink;
And down the borders, well I know,
The poppy and the pansy blow . . .
Oh! there the chestnuts, summer through,
Beside the river make for you
A tunnel of green gloom, and sleep
Deeply above; and green and deep
The stream mysterious glides beneath,
Green as a dream and deep as death.
– Oh, damn! I know it! and I know
How the May fields all golden show,
And when the day is young and sweet,
Gild gloriously the bare feet
That run to bathe . . .
                                    Du lieber Gott!

Here am I, sweating, sick, and hot,
And there the shadowed waters fresh
Lean up to embrace the naked flesh.
Temperamentvoll German Jews
Drink beer around; – and *there* the dews
Are soft beneath a morn of gold.
Here tulips bloom as they are told;
Unkempt about those hedges blows
An English unofficial rose;
And there the unregulated sun
Slopes down to rest when day is done,
And wakes a vague unpunctual star,
A slippered Hesper; and there are
Meads towards Haslingfield and Coton
Where *das Betreten*'s not *verboten.*

εἴθε γενοίμην . . . would I were
In Grantchester, in Grantchester! –
Some, it may be, can get in touch

With Nature there, or Earth, or such.
And clever modern men have seen
A Faun a-peeping through the green,
And felt the Classics were not dead,
To glimpse a Naiad's reedy head,
Or hear the Goat-foot piping low: . . .
But these are things I do not know.
I only know that you may lie
Day-long and watch the Cambridge sky,
And, flower-lulled in sleepy grass,
Hear the cool lapse of hours pass,
Until the centuries blend and blur
In Grantchester, in Grantchester . . .
Still in the dawnlit waters cool
His ghostly Lordship swims his pool,
And tries the strokes, essays the tricks,
Long learnt on Hellespont, or Styx.
Dan Chaucer hears his river still
Chatter beneath a phantom mill.
Tennyson notes, with studious eye,
How Cambridge waters hurry by . . .
And in that garden, black and white,
Creep whispers through the grass all night;
And spectral dance, before the dawn,
A hundred Vicars down the lawn;
Curates, long dust, will come and go
On lissom, clerical, printless toe;
And oft between the boughs is seen
The sly shade of a Rural Dean . . .
Till, at a shiver in the skies,
Vanishing with Satanic cries,
The prim ecclesiastic rout
Leaves but a startled sleeper-out,
Grey heavens, the first bird's drowsy calls,
The falling house that never falls.

God! I will pack, and take a train,
And get me to England once again!
For England's the one land, I know,
Where men with Splendid Hearts may go;
And Cambridgeshire, of all England,
The shire for Men who Understand;

And of *that* district I prefer
The lovely hamlet Grantchester.
For Cambridge people rarely smile,
Being urban, squat, and packed with guile;
And Royston men in the far South
Are black and fierce and strange of mouth;
At Over they fling oaths at one,
And worse than oaths at Trumpington,
And Ditton girls are mean and dirty,
And there's none in Harston under thirty,
And folks in Shelford and those parts
Have twisted lips and twisted hearts,
And Barton men make Cockney rhymes,
And Coton's full of nameless crimes,
And things are done you'd not believe
At Madingley, on Christmas Eve.
Strong men have run for miles and miles,
When one from Cherry Hinton smiles;
Strong men have blanched, and shot their wives,
Rather than send them to St Ives;
Strong men have cried like babes, bydam,
To hear what happened at Babraham.
But Grantchester! ah, Grantchester!
There's peace and holy quiet there,
Great clouds along pacific skies,
And men and women with straight eyes,
Lithe children lovelier than a dream,
A bosky wood, a slumbrous stream,
And little kindly winds that creep
Round twilight corners, half asleep.
In Grantchester their skins are white;
They bathe by day, they bathe by night;
The women there do all they ought;
The men observe the Rules of Thought.
They love the Good; they worship Truth;
They laugh uproariously in youth;
(And when they get to feeling old,
They up and shoot themselves, I'm told) . . .
  Ah God! to see the branches stir
Across the moon at Grantchester!
To smell the thrilling-sweet and rotten
Unforgettable, unforgotten

River-smell, and hear the breeze
Sobbing in the little trees.
Say, do the elm-clumps greatly stand
Still guardians of that holy land?
The chestnuts shade, in reverend dream,
The yet unacademic stream?
Is dawn a secret shy and cold
Anadyomene, silver-gold?
And sunset still a golden sea
From Haslingfield to Madingley?
And after, ere the night is born,
Do hares come out about the corn?
Oh, is the water sweet and cool,
Gentle and brown, above the pool?
And laughs the immortal river still
Under the mill, under the mill?
Say, is there Beauty yet to find?
And Certainty? and Quiet kind?
Deep meadows yet, for to forget
The lies, the truths, and pain? . . . oh! yet
Stands the Church clock at ten to three?
And is there honey still for tea?

RUPERT BROOKE
(Café des Westens, Berlin, May 1912)

'Fear no more the heat o' the sun'

FEAR no more the heat o' the sun,
    Nor the furious winter's rages;
Thou thy worldly task hast done,
    Home art gone, and ta'en thy wages;
Golden lads and girls all must
    As chimney-sweepers, come to dust.

Fear no more the frown o' the great,
    Thou art past the tyrant's stroke:
Care no more to clothe and eat;
    To thee the reed is as the oak;
The sceptre, learning, physic, must
    All follow this, and come to dust.

Fear no more the lightning-flash,
    Nor the all-dreaded thunder-stone;
Fear not slander, censure rash;
    Thou hast finish'd joy and moan:
All lovers young, all lovers must
    Consign to thee, and come to dust.

No exorcizer harm thee!
    Nor no witchcraft charm thee!
Ghost unlaid forbear thee!
    Nothing ill come near thee!
Quiet consummation have;
    And renowned be thy grave!

WILLIAM SHAKESPEARE
from Cymbeline, IV.ii

Daffodils

I WANDER'D lonely as a cloud
   That floats on high o'er vales and hills,
When all at once I saw a crowd,
   A host, of golden daffodils;
Beside the lake, beneath the trees,
Fluttering and dancing in the breeze.

Continuous as the stars that shine
   And twinkle on the Milky Way,
They stretch'd in never-ending line
   Along the margin of a bay:
Ten thousand saw I at a glance,
Tossing their heads in sprightly dance.

The waves beside them danced, but they
   Outdid the sparkling waves in glee:
A poet could not but be gay,
   In such a jocund company:
I gazed – and gazed – but little thought
What wealth the show to me had brought:

For oft, when on my couch I lie
   In vacant or in pensive mood,
They flash upon that inward eye
   Which is the bliss of solitude;
And then my heart with pleasure fills,
And dances with the daffodils.

WILLIAM WORDSWORTH

Upon Westminster Bridge

EARTH has not anything to show more fair;
   Dull would he be of soul who could pass by
   A sight so touching in its majesty;
This City now doth, like a garment, wear
The beauty of the morning; silent, bare,
   Ships, towers, domes, theatres, and temples lie
   Open unto the fields, and to the sky;
All bright and glittering in the smokeless air.
Never did sun more beautifully steep
   In his first splendour, valley, rock, or hill;
Ne'er saw I, never felt, a calm so deep!
   The river glideth at his own sweet will:
Dear God! the very houses seem asleep:
   And all that mighty heart is lying still!

WILLIAM WORDSWORTH

'Do not go gentle into that good night'

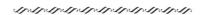

Do not go gentle into that good night,
Old age should burn and rave at close of day;
Rage, rage against the dying of the light.

Though wise men at their end know dark is right,
Because their words had forked no lightning they
Do not go gentle into that good night.

Good men, the last wave by, crying how bright
Their frail deeds might have danced in a green bay,
Rage, rage against the dying of the light.

Wild men who caught and sang the sun in flight,
And learn, too late, they grieved it on its way,
Do not go gentle into that good night.

Grave men, near death, who see with blinding sight
Blind eyes could blaze like meteors and be gay,
Rage, rage against the dying of the light.

And you, my father, there on the sad height,
Curse, bless, me now with your fierce tears, I pray.
Do not go gentle into that good night.
Rage, rage against the dying of the light.

DYLAN THOMAS

from *Lycidas*

A lament for a friend drowned in his passage
from Chester on the Irish Seas, 1637

YE valleys low where the mild whispers use,
Of shades and wanton winds, and gushing brooks,
On whose fresh lap the swart star sparely looks,
Throw hither all your quaint enamelled eyes,
That on the green turf suck the honied showers,
And purple all the ground with vernal flowers.
Bring the rathe primrose that forsaken dies,
The tufted crow-toe, and pale jessamine,
The white pink, and the pansy freaked with jet,
The glowing violet,
The musk-rose, and the well attir'd woodbine,
With cowslips wan that hang the pensive head,
And every flower that sad embroidery wears:
Bid amaranthus all his beauty shed,
And daffadillies fill their cups with tears,
To strew the laureate hearse where Lycid lies.
For so to interpose a little ease,
Let our frail thoughts dally with false surmise.
Ay me! Whilst thee the shores, and sounding seas
Wash far away, where'er thy bones are hurled,
Whether beyond the stormy Hebrides,
Where thou perhaps under the whelming tide
Visit'st the bottom of the monstrous world;
Or whether thou to our moist vows denied,
Sleep'st by the fable of Bellerus old,
Where the great vision of the guarded mount
Looks toward Namancos and Bayona's hold;
Look homeward angel now, and melt with ruth.
And, O ye dolphins, waft the hapless youth.
    Weep no more, woeful shepherds weep no more,
For Lycidas your sorrow is not dead,
Sunk though he be beneath the wat'ry floor,
So sinks the day-star in the ocean bed,
And yet anon repairs his drooping head,
And tricks his beams, and with new spangled ore,

Flames in the forehead of the morning sky:
So Lycidas sunk low, but mounted high,
Through the dear might of him that walked the waves
Where other groves, and other streams along,
With nectar pure his oozy locks he laves,
And hears the unexpressive nuptial song,
In the blest kingdoms meek of joy and love.
There entertain him all the saints above,
In solemn troops, and sweet societies
That sing, and singing in their glory move,
And wipe the tears for ever from his eyes.
Now Lycidas the shepherds weep no more;
Henceforth thou art the genius of the shore,
In thy large recompense, and shalt be good
To all that wander in that perilous flood.

JOHN MILTON

from *The Song of Hiawatha*

By the shores of Gitche Gumee,
By the shining Big-Sea-Water,
Stood the wigwam of Nokomis,
Daughter of the Moon, Nokomis.
Dark behind it rose the forest,
Rose the black and gloomy pine-trees,
Rose the firs with cones upon them;
Bright before it beat the water,
Beat the clear and sunny water,
Beat the shining Big-Sea-Water.
  There the wrinkled old Nokomis
Nursed the little Hiawatha,
Rocked him in his linden cradle,
Bedded soft with moss and rushes,
Safely bound with reindeer sinews;
Stilled his fretful wail by saying,
'Hush! the Naked Bear will hear thee!'
Lulled him into slumber, singing,
'Ewa-yea! my little owlet!'
Who is this, that lights the wigwam?
With his great eyes lights the wigwam?
Ewa-yea! my little owlet!
  Many things Nokomis taught him
Of the stars that shine in heaven;
Showed him Ishkoodah, the comet,
Ishkoodah, with fiery tresses;
Showed the Death-Dance of the spirits,
Warriors with their plumes and war-clubs,
Flaring far away to northward
In the frosty nights of Winter;
Showed the broad white road in heaven,
Pathway of the ghosts, the shadows,
Running straight across the heavens,
Crowded with the ghosts, the shadows.
  At the door on summer evenings
Sat the little Hiawatha;
Heard the whispering of the pine-trees,

Heard the lapping of the waters,
Sounds of music, words of wonder;
'Minne-wawa!' said the pine-trees,
'Mudway-aushka!' said the water.
    Saw the firefly, Wah-wah-taysee,
Flitting through the dusk of evening,
With the twinkle of its candle
Lighting up the brakes and bushes,
And he sang the song of children,
Sang the song Nokomis taught him:
'Wah-wah-taysee, little firefly,
Little, flitting, white-fire insect,
Little, dancing, white-fire creature,
Light me with your little candle,
Ere upon my bed I lay me,
Ere in sleep I close my eyelids!'
    Saw the moon rise from the water,
Rippling, rounding from the water,
Saw the flecks and shadows on it,
Whispered, 'What is that, Nokomis?'
And the good Nokomis answered:
'Once a warrior, very angry,
Seized his grandmother, and threw her
Up into the sky at midnight;
Right against the moon he threw her;
'Tis her body that you see there.'
    Saw the rainbow in the heaven,
In the eastern sky, the rainbow,
Whispered, 'What is that, Nokomis?'
And the good Nokomis answered:
''Tis the heaven of flowers you see there;
All the wild-flowers of the forest,
All the lilies of the prairie,
When on earth they fade and perish,
Blossom in that heaven above us.'
    When he heard the owls at midnight,
Hooting, laughing in the forest,
'What is that?' he cried in terror,
'What is that,' he said, 'Nokomis?'
And the good Nokomis answered:
'That is but the owl and owlet,
Talking in their native language,

Talking, scolding at each other.'
   Then the little Hiawatha
Learned of every bird its language,
Learned their names and all their secrets,
How they built their nests in Summer,
Where they hid themselves in Winter,
Talked with them whene'er he met them,
Called them 'Hiawatha's Chickens.'
   Of all beasts he learned the language,
Learned their names and all their secrets,
How the beavers built their lodges,
Where the squirrels hid their acorns,
How the reindeer ran so swiftly,
Why the rabbit was so timid,
Talked with them whene'er he met them,
Called them 'Hiawatha's Brothers.'

H. W. LONGFELLOW

from *Under Milk Wood*

ༀༀ

FIRST VOICE

> In the blind-drawn dark dining-room of School
> House, dusty and echoing as a dining-room in a vault,
> Mr and Mrs Pugh are silent over cold grey cottage pie.
> Mr Pugh reads, as he forks the shroud meat in, from
> *Lives of the Great Poisoners*. He has bound a plain
> brown-paper cover round the book. Slyly, between
> slow mouthfuls, he sidespies up at Mrs Pugh, poisons
> her with his eye, then goes on reading. He underlines
> certain passages and smiles in secret.

MRS PUGH

> Persons with manners do not read at table,

FIRST VOICE

> says Mrs Pugh. She swallows a digestive tablet as big
> as a horse-pill, washing it down with clouded peasoup
> water.
>
> > [*Pause*

MRS PUGH

> Some persons were brought up in pigsties.

MR PUGH

> Pigs don't read at table, dear.

FIRST VOICE

> Bitterly she flicks dust from the broken cruet. It
> settles on the pie in a thin gnat-rain.

MR PUGH

> Pigs can't read, my dear.

MRS PUGH

> I know one who can.

FIRST VOICE

> Alone in the hissing laboratory of his wishes, Mr
> Pugh minces among bad vats and jeroboams, tiptoes
> through spinneys of murdering herbs, agony dancing
> in his crucibles, and mixes especially for Mrs Pugh a
> venomous porridge unknown to toxicologists which

will scald and viper through her until her ears fall
off like figs, her toes grow big and black as balloons,
and steam comes screaming out of her navel.

MR PUGH

Who know best, dear,

FIRST VOICE

says Mr Pugh, and quick as a flash he ducks her in
rat soup.

MRS PUGH

What's that book by your trough, Mr Pugh?

MR PUGH

It's a theological work, my dear. *Lives of the Great
Saints.*

*   *   *

MRS PUGH

Persons with manners,

SECOND VOICE

snaps Mrs cold Pugh,

MRS PUGH

do not nod at table.

FIRST VOICE

Mr Pugh cringes awake. He puts on a soft-soaping
smile: it is sad and grey under his nicotine-eggyellow
weeping walrus Victorian moustache worn thick and
long in memory of Doctor Crippen.

MRS PUGH

You should wait until you retire to your sty,

SECOND VOICE

says Mrs Pugh, sweet as a razor. His fawning
measly quarter-smile freezes. Sly and silent, he foxes
into his chemist's den and there, in a hiss and prussic
circle of cauldrons and phials brimful with pox and
the Black Death, cooks up a fricassee of deadly night-
shade, nicotine, hot frog, cyanide and bat-spit for his
needling stalactite hag and bednag of a pokerbacked
nutcracker wife.

DYLAN THOMAS

The Burial of Sir John Moore
after Corunna

Not a drum was heard, not a funeral note,
   As his corse to the rampart we hurried;
Not a soldier discharged his farewell shot
   O'er the grave where our hero we buried.

We buried him darkly at dead of night,
   The sods with our bayonets turning,
By the struggling moonbeam's misty light
   And the lanthorn dimly burning.

No useless coffin enclosed his breast,
   Not in sheet or in shroud we wound him;
But he lay like a warrior taking his rest
   With his martial cloak around him.

Few and short were the prayers we said,
   And we spoke not a word of sorrow;
But we steadfastly gazed on the face that was dead,
   And we bitterly thought of the morrow.

We thought, as we hollow'd his narrow bed
   And smooth'd down his lonely pillow,
That the foe and the stranger would tread o'er his head,
   And we far away on the billow!

Lightly they'll talk of the spirit that's gone,
   And o'er his cold ashes upbraid him –
But little he'll reck, if they let him sleep on
   In the grave where a Briton has laid him.

But half of our heavy task was done
   When the clock struck the hour for retiring;
And we heard the distant and random gun
   That the foe was sullenly firing.

Slowly and sadly we laid him down,
   From the field of his fame fresh and gory;
We carved not a line, and we raised not a stone,
   But we left him alone with his glory.

Charles Wolfe

Pied Beauty

GLORY be to God for dappled things –
   For skies of couple-colour as a brinded cow;
      For rose-moles all in stipple upon trout that swim;
Fresh-firecoal chestnut-falls; finches' wings;
   Landscape plotted and pieced – fold, fallow, and plough;
      And áll trádes, their gear and tackle and trim.

All things counter, original, spare, strange;
   Whatever is fickle, freckled (who knows how?)
      With swift, slow; sweet, sour; adazzle, dim;
He fathers-forth whose beauty is past change:
                                       Praise him.

                              GERARD MANLEY HOPKINS

The Leaden Echo and the Golden Echo

(Maidens' song from St Winefred's Well)

THE LEADEN ECHO

How to kéep – is there ány any, is there none such, nowhere
    known some, bow or brooch or braid or brace, láce,
    latch or catch or key to keep
Back beauty, keep it, beauty, beauty, beauty, . . . from
    vanishing away?
Ó is there no frowning of these wrinkles, rankèd wrinkles
    deep,
Dówn? no waving off of these most mournful messengers,
    still messengers, sad and stealing messengers of grey?
No there's none, there's none, O no there's none.
Nor can you long be, what you now are, called fair,
Do what you may do, what, do what you may,
And wisdom is early to despair:
Be beginning; since, no, nothing can be done
To keep at bay
Age and age's evils, hoar hair,
Ruck and wrinkle, drooping, dying, death's worst, winding
    sheets, tombs and worms and tumbling to decay;
So be beginning, be beginning to despair.
O there's none; no no no there's none:
Be beginning to despair, to despair,
Despair, despair, despair, despair.

THE GOLDEN ECHO

               Spare!
There ís one, yes I have one (Hush there!);
Only not within seeing of the sun,
Not within the singeing of the strong sun,
Tall sun's tingeing, or treacherous the tainting of the earth's air,
Somewhere elsewhere there is ah well where! one,
Óne. Yes I can tell such a key, I do know such a place,

Where whatever's prized and passes of us, everything that's fresh and
    fast flying of us, seems to us sweet of us and swiftly away with,
    done away with, undone,
Undone, done with, soon done with, and yet dearly and dangerously
    sweet
Of us, the wimpled-water-dimpled, not-by-morning-matchèd face,
The flower of beauty, fleece of beauty, too too apt to, ah! to fleet,
Never fleets móre, fastened with the tenderest truth
To its own best being and its loveliness of youth: it is an ever-
    lastingness of, O it is an all youth!
Come then, your ways and airs and looks, locks, maiden gear,
    gallantry and gaiety and grace,
Winning ways, airs innocent, maiden manners, sweet looks, loose
    locks, long locks, lovelocks, gaygear, going gallant, girlgrace –
Resign them, sign them, seal them, send them, motion them with
    breath,
And with sighs soaring, soaring síghs deliver
Them; beauty-in-the-ghost, deliver it, early now, long before death
Give beauty back, beauty, beauty, beauty, back to God, beauty's self
    and beauty's giver.
See; not a hair is, not an eyelash, not the least lash lost; every hair
Is, hair of the head, numbered.
Nay, what we had lighthanded left in surly the mere mould
Will have waked and have waxed and have walked with the wind what
    while we slept,
This side, that side hurling a heavyheaded hundredfold
What while we, while we slumbered.
O then, weary then whý should we tread? O why are we so haggard at
    the heart, so care-coiled, care-killed, so fagged, so fashed, so
    cogged, so cumbered,
When the thing we freely fórfeit is kept with fonder a care,
Fonder a care kept than we could have kept it, kept
Far with fonder a care (and we, we should have lost it) finer, fonder
A care kept. – Where kept? do but tell us where kept, where. –
Yonder. – What high as that! We follow, now we follow. – Yonder,
    yes yonder, yonder,
Yonder.

GERARD MANLEY HOPKINS

from *Paradise Lost*

Of Man's first disobedience, and the fruit
Of that forbidden tree, whose mortal taste
Brought death into the world, and all our woe,
With loss of Eden, till one greater Man
Restore us, and regain the blissful seat,
Sing, Heavenly Muse, that on the secret top
Of Oreb, or of Sinai, didst inspire
That shepherd, who first taught the chosen seed,
In the beginning how the Heavens and Earth
Rose out of Chaos; or if Sion hill
Delight thee more, and Siloa's brook that flowed
Fast by the oracle of God, I thence
Invoke thy aid to my adventurous song,
That with no middle flight intends to soar
Above the Aonian mount, while it pursues
Things unattempted yet in prose or rhyme.
And chiefly thou, O Spirit, that dost prefer
Before all temples the upright heart and pure,
Instruct me, for thou know'st; thou from the first
Wast present, and with mighty wings outspread
Dove-like sat'st brooding on the vast abyss
And mad'st it pregnant: what in me is dark
Illumine, what is low raise and support;
That to the height of this great argument
I may assert Eternal Providence,
And justify the ways of God to men.
    Say first, for Heaven hides nothing from thy view,
Nor the deep tract of Hell, say first what cause
Moved our grand parents in that happy state,
Favoured of Heaven so highly, to fall off
From their Creator, and transgress his will
For one restraint, lords of the world besides?
Who first seduced them to that foul revolt?
The infernal Serpent; he it was, whose guile,
Stirred up with envy and revenge, deceived
The mother of mankind, what time his pride
Had cast him out from Heaven, with all his host

Of rebel angels, by whose aid aspiring
To set himself in glory above his peers,
He trusted to have equalled the Most High,
If he opposed; and with ambitious aim
Against the throne and monarchy of God,
Raised impious war in Heaven and battle proud
With vain attempt. Him the Almighty Power
Hurled headlong flaming from the ethereal sky
With hideous ruin and combustion down
To bottomless perdition, there to dwell
In adamantine chains and penal fire,
Who durst defy the Omnipotent to arms.
Nine times the space that measures day and night
To mortal men, he with his horrid crew
Lay vanquished, rolling in the fiery gulf
Confounded though immortal. But his doom
Reserved him to more wrath; for now the thought
Both of lost happiness and lasting pain
Torments him; round he throws his baleful eyes,
That witnessed huge affliction and dismay
Mixed with obdurate pride and steadfast hate.
At once as far as angels ken he views
The dismal situation waste and wild:
A dungeon horrible, on all sides round
As one great furnace flamed, yet from those flames
No light, but rather darkness visible
Served only to discover sights of woe,
Regions of sorrow, doleful shades, where peace
And rest can never dwell, hope never comes
That comes to all; but torture without end
Still urges, and a fiery deluge, fed
With ever-burning sulphur unconsumed:
Such place Eternal Justice had prepared
For those rebellious, here their prison ordained
In utter darkness, and their portion set
As far removed from God and light of Heaven
As from the center thrice to the utmost pole.

JOHN MILTON

[82]

from *The Rubáiyát of Omar Khayyám*

AWAKE! for Morning in the Bowl of Night
Has flung the Stone that puts the Stars to Flight:
   And Lo! the Hunter of the East has caught
The Sultán's Turret in a Noose of Light.

Dreaming when Dawn's Left Hand was in the Sky
I heard a Voice within the Tavern cry,
   'Awake, my Little ones, and fill the Cup
Before Life's Liquor in its Cup be dry.'

And, as the Cock crew, those who stood before
The Tavern shouted – 'Open then the door!
   You know how little while we have to stay,
And, once departed, may return no more.'

Now the New Year reviving old Desires,
The thoughtful Soul to Solitude retires,
   Where the White Hand of Moses on the bough
Puts out, and Jesus from the Ground suspires.

Irám indeed is gone with all its Rose,
And Jamshýd's Sev'n-ring'd Cup where no one knows;
   But still the Vine her ancient Ruby yields,
And still a Garden by the Water blows.

And David's Lips are lock't; but in divine
High piping Pehleví, with 'Wine! Wine! Wine!
   Red Wine!' – the Nightingale cries to the Rose
That yellow Cheek of hers to incarnadine.

Come, fill the Cup, and in the Fire of Spring
The Winter Garment of Repentance fling:
   The Bird of Time has but a little way
To fly – and Lo! the Bird is on the Wing.

And look – a thousand Blossoms with the Day
Woke – and a thousand scatter'd into Clay:
   And this first Summer Month that brings the Rose
Shall take Jamshýd and Kaikobád away.

[83]

But come with old Khayyám, and leave the Lot
Of Kaikobád and Kaikhosrú forgot:
   Let Rustum lay about him as he will,
Or Hátim Tai cry Supper – heed them not.

With me along some Strip of Herbage strown
That just divides the desert from the sown,
   Where name of Slave and Sultán scarce is known,
And pity Sultán Máhmúd on his Throne

Here with a Loaf of Bread beneath the Bough,
A Flask of Wine, a Book of Verse – and Thou
   Beside me singing in the Wilderness –
And Wilderness is Paradise enow.

'How sweet is mortal Sovranty!' – think some:
Others – 'How blest the Paradise to come!'
   Ah, take the Cash in hand and waive the Rest;
Oh, the brave Music of a *distant* Drum!

EDWARD FITZGERALD

Sonnet 73

THAT time of year thou mayst in me behold
When yellow leaves, or none, or few, do hang
Upon those boughs which shake against the cold,
Bare ruined choirs where late the sweet birds sang.
In me thou see'st the twilight of such day
As after sunset fadeth in the west,
Which by and by black night doth take away,
Death's second self that seals up all in rest.
In me thou see'st the glowing of such fire
That on the ashes of his youth doth lie
As the death-bed whereon It must expire,
Consum'd with that which it was nourished by.
    This thou perceiv'st, which makes thy love more strong,
    To love that well which thou must leave ere long.

WILLIAM SHAKESPEARE

A Toccata of Galuppi's

Oh, Galuppi, Baldassaro, this is very sad to find!
I can hardly misconceive you; it would prove me deaf and blind;
But although I give you credit, 'tis with such a heavy mind!

Here you come with your old music, and here's all the good it brings.
What, they lived once thus at Venice, where the merchants were the
     kings,
Where St Mark's is, where the Doges used to wed the sea with rings?

Ay, because the sea's the street there; and 'tis arched by . . . what you
     call
. . . Shylock's bridge with houses on it, where they kept the carnival!
I was never out of England – it's as if I saw it all!

Did young people take their pleasure when the sea was warm in May?
Balls and masks begun at midnight, burning ever to mid-day,
When they made up fresh adventures for the morrow, do you say?

Was a lady such a lady, cheeks so round and lips so red, –
On her neck the small face buoyant, like a bell-flower on its bed,
O'er the breast's superb abundance where a man might base his head?

Well (and it was graceful of them) they'd break talk off and afford
– She, to bite her mask's black velvet, he to finger on his sword,
While you sat and played Toccatas, stately at the clavichord?

What? Those lesser thirds so plaintive, sixths diminished, sigh on sigh,
Told them something? Those suspensions, those solutions – 'Must we
     die?'
Those commiserating sevenths – 'Life might last! we can but try!'

'Were you happy?' – 'Yes.' 'And are you still as happy?' – 'Yes – and
     you?'
– 'Then more kisses' – 'Did *I* stop them, when a million seemed so
     few?'
Hark – the dominant's persistence, till it must be answered to.

So an octave struck the answer. Oh, they praised you, I dare say!
'Brave Galuppi! that was music! good alike at grave and gay!
I can always leave off talking, when I hear a master play.'

Then they left you for their pleasure: till in due time, one by one,
Some with lives that came to nothing, some with deeds as well
      undone,
Death came tacitly and took them where they never see the sun.

But when I sit down to reason, – think to take my stand nor swerve
Till I triumph o'er a secret wrung from nature's close reserve,
In you come with your cold music, till I creep thro' every nerve,

Yes, you, like a ghostly cricket, creaking where a house was burned –
'Dust and ashes, dead and done with, Venice spent what Venice
      earned!
The soul, doubtless, is immortal – where a soul can be discerned.

'Yours for instance, you know physics, something of geology,
Mathematics are your pastime; souls shall rise in their degree;
Butterflies may dread extinction, – you'll not die, it cannot be!

'As for Venice and its people, merely born to bloom and drop,
Here on earth they bore their fruitage, mirth and folly were the crop,
What of soul was left, I wonder, when the kissing had to stop?

'Dust and ashes!' So you creak it, and I want the heart to scold.
Dear dead women, with such hair, too – what's become of all the gold
Used to hang and brush their bosoms? I feel chilly and grown old.

ROBERT BROWNING

Exposure

Our brains ache, in the merciless iced east winds that knive us . . .
Wearied we keep awake because the night is silent . . .
Low, drooping flares confuse our memory of the salient . . .
Worried by silence, sentries whisper, curious, nervous,
　　　　But nothing happens.

Watching, we hear the mad gusts tugging on the wire,
Like twitching agonies of men among its brambles.
Northward, incessantly, the flickering gunnery rumbles,
Far off, like a dull rumour of some other war.
　　　　What are we doing here?

The poignant misery of dawn begins to grow . . .
We only know war lasts, rain soaks, and clouds sag stormy.
Dawn massing in the east her melancholy army
Attacks once more in ranks on shivering ranks of gray,
　　　　But nothing happens.

Sudden successive flights of bullets streak the silence.
Less deadly than the air that shudders black with snow,
With sidelong flowing flakes that flock, pause, and renew,
We watch them wandering up and down the wind's nonchalance,
　　　　But nothing happens.

Pale flakes with fingering stealth come feeling for our faces –
We cringe in holes, back on forgotten dreams, and stare, snow-dazed,
Deep into grassier ditches. So we drowse, sun-dozed,
Littered with blossoms trickling where the blackbird fusses.
　　　　Is it that we are dying?

Slowly our ghosts drag home: glimpsing the sunk fires, glozed
With crusted dark-red jewels; crickets jingle there;
For hours the innocent mice rejoice: the house is theirs;
Shutters and doors, all closed: on us the doors are closed, –
　　　　We turn back to our dying.

Since we believe not otherwise can kind fires burn;
Nor ever suns smile true on child, or field, or fruit.
For God's invincible spring our love is made afraid;
Therefore, not loath, we lie out here; therefore were born,
      For love of God seems dying.

To-night, His frost will fasten on this mud and us,
Shrivelling many hands, puckering foreheads crisp.
The burying-party, picks and shovels in their shaking grasp,
Pause over half-known faces. All their eyes are ice,
      But nothing happens.

WILFRED OWEN

He Wishes for
the Cloths of Heaven

HAD I the heavens' embroidered cloths,
Enwrought with golden and silver light,
The blue and the dim and the dark cloths
Of night and light and the half-light,
I would spread the cloths under your feet:
But I, being poor, have only my dreams;
I have spread my dreams under your feet;
Tread softly because you tread on my dreams.

W. B. YEATS

Lullaby: 'Lay your sleeping head, my love'

Lay your sleeping head, my love,
Human on my faithless arm;
Time and fevers burn away
Individual beauty from
Thoughtful children, and the grave
Proves the child ephemeral:
But in my arms till break of day
Let the living creature lie,
Mortal, guilty, but to me
The entirely beautiful.

Soul and body have no bounds:
To lovers as they lie upon
Her tolerant enchanted slope
In their ordinary swoon,
Grave the vision Venus sends
Of supernatural sympathy,
Universal love and hope;
While an abstract insight wakes
Among the glaciers and the rocks
The hermit's carnal ecstasy.

Certainty, fidelity
On the stroke of midnight pass
Like vibrations of a bell
And fashionable madmen raise
Their pedantic boring cry:
Every farthing of the cost,
All the dreaded cards foretell,
Shall be paid, but from this night
Not a whisper, not a thought,
Not a kiss nor look be lost.

Beauty, midnight, vision dies:
Let the winds of dawn that blow
Softly round your dreaming head
Such a day of welcome show
Eye and knocking heart may bless,
Find the mortal world enough;
Noons of dryness find you fed
By the involuntary powers,
Nights of insult let you pass
Watched by every human love.

W. H. AUDEN

The Windhover

To Christ our Lord

I CAUGHT this morning morning's minion, king-
   dom of daylight's dauphin, dapple-dawn-drawn
     Falcon, in his riding
   Of the rolling level underneath him steady air, and striding
High there, how he rung upon the rein of a wimpling wing
In his ecstasy! then off, off forth on swing,
   As a skate's heel sweeps smooth on a bow-bend: the hurl and
     gliding
   Rebuffed the big wind. My heart in hiding
Stirred for a bird, – the achieve of, the mastery of the thing!

Brute beauty and valour and act, oh, air, pride, plume, here
   Buckle! AND the fire that breaks from thee then, a billion
Times told lovelier, more dangerous, O my chevalier!

   No wonder of it: shéer plód makes plough down sillion
Shine, and blue-bleak embers, ah my dear,
   Fall, gall themselves, and gash gold-vermilion.

GERARD MANLEY HOPKINS

Dulce Et Decorum Est

BENT double, like old beggars under sacks,
Knock-kneed, coughing like hags, we cursed through sludge,
Till on the haunting flares we turned our backs
And towards our distant rest began to trudge.
Men marched asleep. Many had lost their boots
But limped on, blood-shod. All went lame; all blind;
Drunk with fatigue; deaf even to the hoots
Of gas shells dropping softly behind.

Gas! GAS! Quick, boys! – An ecstasy of fumbling,
Fitting the clumsy helmets just in time;
But someone still was yelling out and stumbling,
And flound'ring like a man in fire or lime . . .
Dim, through the misty panes and thick green light,
As under a green sea, I saw him drowning.

In all my dreams, before my helpless sight,
He plunges at me, guttering, choking, drowning.

If in some smothering dreams you too could pace
Behind the wagon that we flung him in,
And watch the white eyes writhing in his face,
His hanging face, like a devil's sick of sin;
If you could hear, at every jolt, the blood
Come gargling from the froth-corrupted lungs,
Obscene as cancer, bitter as the cud
Of vile, incurable sores on innocent tongues, –
My friend, you would not tell with such high zest
To children ardent for some desperate glory,
The old Lie: Dulce et decorum est
Pro patria mori.

WILFRED OWEN

On his Blindness

WHEN I consider how my light is spent,
   Ere half my days, in this dark world and wide,
   And that one talent which is death to hide,
Lodged with me useless, though my soul more bent
To serve therewith my Maker, and present
   My true account, lest He returning chide;
   'Doth God exact day-labour, light denied?'
I fondly ask: but patience, to prevent
That murmur, soon replies 'God doth not need
   Either man's work, or his own gifts: who best
     Bear his mild yoke, they serve him best; his state
Is kingly. Thousands at his bidding speed,
   And post o'er land and ocean without rest;
     They also serve who only stand and wait.'

JOHN MILTON

The Soldier

IF I should die, think only this of me:
 That there's some corner of a foreign field
That is for ever England. There shall be
 In that rich earth a richer dust concealed;
A dust whom England bore, shaped, made aware,
 Gave, once, her flowers to love, her ways to roam,
A body of England's, breathing English air,
 Washed by the rivers, blest by suns of home.

And think, this heart, all evil shed away,
 A pulse in the eternal mind, no less
  Gives somewhere back the thoughts by England given;
Her sights and sounds; dreams happy as her day;
 And laughter, learnt of friends; and gentleness,
  In hearts at peace, under an English heaven.

RUPERT BROOKE
November–December 1914

Sonnet 116

ಬಬ

Let me not to the marriage of true minds
Admit impediments; love is not love
Which alters when it alteration finds,
Or bends with the remover to remove.
O no, it is an ever-fixèd mark
That looks on tempests and is never shaken;
It is the star to every wandering bark,
Whose worth's unknown although his height be taken.
Love's not Time's fool, though rosy lips and cheeks
Within his bending sickle's compass come;
Love alters not with his brief hours and weeks,
But bears it out even to the edge of doom.
    If this be error and upon me proved,
    I never writ, nor no man ever loved.

William Shakespeare

Jim

THERE was a Boy whose name was Jim;
His Friends were very good to him.
They gave him Tea, and Cakes, and Jam.
And slices of delicious Ham,
And Chocolate with pink inside,
And little Tricycles to ride,
And read him Stories through and through,
And even took him to the Zoo –
But there it was the dreadful Fate
Befell him, which I now relate.

You know – at least you ought to know,
For I have often told you so –
That Children never are allowed
To leave their Nurses in a Crowd;
Now this was Jim's especial Foible,
He ran away when he was able,
And on this inauspicious day
He slipped his hand and ran away!

He hadn't gone a yard when – Bang!
With open Jaws, a Lion sprang,
And hungrily began to eat
The Boy: beginning at his feet.
Now, just imagine how it feels
When first your toes and then your heels,
And then by gradual degrees,
Your shins and ankles, calves and knees,
Are slowly eaten, bit by bit.
No wonder Jim detested it!
No wonder that he shouted 'Hi!'

The Honest Keeper heard his cry,
Though very fat he almost ran
To help the little gentleman.
'Ponto!' he ordered as he came
(For Ponto was the Lion's name),
'Ponto!' he cried, with angry Frown,

'Let go, Sir! Down, Sir! Put it down!'
The Lion made a sudden stop,
He let the Dainty Morsel drop,
And slunk reluctant to his Cage,
Snarling with Disappointed Rage.
But when he bent him over Jim,
The Honest Keeper's Eyes were dim.
The Lion having reached his Head,
The Miserable Boy was dead!

When Nurse informed his Parents, they
Were more Concerned than I can say: –
His Mother, as she dried her eyes,
Said, 'Well – it gives me no surprise,
He would not do as he was told!'
His Father, who was self-controlled,
Bade all the children round attend
To James's miserable end,
And always keep a-hold of Nurse
For fear of finding something worse.

HILAIRE BELLOC

Sonnet 30

WHEN to the sessions of sweet silent thought
I summon up remembrance of things past,
I sigh the lack of many a thing I sought,
And with old woes new wail my dear times waste:
Then can I drown an eye, unus'd to flow,
For precious friends hid in death's dateless night,
And weep afresh love's long since cancelled woe,
And moan the expense of many a vanished sight:
Then can I grieve at grievances foregone,
And heavily from woe to woe tell o'er
The sad account of fore-bemoanèd moan,
Which I new pay as if not paid before.
    But if the while I think on thee, dear friend,
    All losses are restored and sorrows end.

WILLIAM SHAKESPEARE

L'Allegro

Hence, loathèd Melancholy,
    Of Cerberus and blackest Midnight born
In Stygian cave forlorn
    'Mongst horrid shapes, and shrieks, and sights unholy!
Find out some uncouth cell,
    Where brooding Darkness spreads his jealous wings,
And the night-raven sings;
    There, under ebon shades and low-brow'd rocks,
As ragged as thy locks,
    In dark Cimmerian desert ever dwell.
But come, thou Goddess fair and free,
In heaven yclept Euphrosyne,
And by men heart-easing Mirth;
Whom lovely Venus, at a birth,
With two sister Graces more,
To ivy-crownèd Bacchus bore:
Or whether (as some sager sing)
The frolic wind that breathes the spring,
Zephyr, with Aurora playing,
As he met her once a-Maying,
There, on beds of violets blue,
And fresh-blown roses wash'd in dew,
Fill'd her with thee, a daughter fair,
So buxom, blithe, and debonair.

    Haste thee, Nymph, and bring with thee
Jest, and youthful Jollity,
Quips and Cranks and wanton Wiles,
Nods and Becks and wreathèd Smiles,
Such as hang on Hebe's cheek,
And love to live in dimple sleek;
Sport that wrinkled Care derides,
And Laughter holding both his sides.
Come, and trip it, as you go,
On the light fantastic toe;
And in thy right hand lead with thee
The mountain-nymph, sweet Liberty;

And, if I give thee honour due,
Mirth, admit me of thy crew,
To live with her, and live with thee,
In unreprovèd pleasures free;
To hear the lark begin his flight,
And, singing, startle the dull night,
From his watch-tower in the skies,
Till the dappled dawn doth rise;
Then to come, in spite of sorrow,
And at my window bid good-morrow,
Through the sweet-brier or the vine,
Or the twisted eglantine;
While the cock, with lively din,
Scatters the rear of darkness thin;
And to the stack, or the barn-door,
Stoutly struts his dames before:
Oft list'ning how the hounds and horn
Cheerly rouse the slumb'ring morn,
From the side of some hoar hill,
Through the high wood echoing shrill:
Sometime walking, not unseen,
By hedgerow elms, on hillocks green,
Right against the eastern gate
Where the great Sun begins his state,
Robed in flames and amber light,
The clouds in thousand liveries dight;
While the ploughman, near at hand,
Whistles o'er the furrow'd land,
And the milkmaid singeth blithe,
And the mower whets his scythe,
And every shepherd tells his tale
Under the hawthorn in the dale.
Straight mine eye hath caught new pleasures,
Whilst the landskip round it measures:
Russet lawns, and fallows grey,
Where the nibbling flocks do stray;
Mountains on whose barren breast
The labouring clouds do often rest;
Meadows trim with daisies pied,
Shallow brooks, and rivers wide;
Towers and battlements it sees
Bosomed high in tufted trees,

Where perhaps some beauty lies,
The cynosure of neighbouring eyes.
Hard by a cottage chimney smokes
From betwixt two aged oaks,
Where Corydon and Thyrsis met
Are at their savoury dinner set
Of herbs and other country messes,
Which the neat-handed Phillis dresses;
And then in haste her bower she leaves,
With Thestylis to bind the sheaves;
Or, if the earlier season lead,
To the tanned haycock in the mead.
Sometimes, with secure delight,
The upland hamlets will invite,
When the merry bells ring round,
And jocund rebecks sound
To many a youth and many a maid
Dancing in the chequer'd shade,
And young and old come forth to play
On a sunshine holiday,
Till the livelong daylight fail:
Then to the spicy nut-brown ale,
With stories told of many a feat,
How Faery Mab the junkets eat.
She was pinch'd and pull'd, she said;
And he, by Friar's lantern led,
Tells how the drudging goblin sweat
To earn his cream-bowl duly set,
When in one night, ere glimpse of morn,
His shadowy flail hath thresh'd the corn
That ten day-labourers could not end;
Then lies him down, the lubber fiend,
And, stretch'd out all the chimney's length,
Basks at the fire his hairy strength;
And crop-full out of doors he flings,
Ere the first cock his matin rings.
Thus done the tales, to bed they creep,
By whispering winds soon lull'd asleep.
Tower'd cities please us then,
And the busy hum of men,
Where throngs of knights and barons bold,
In weeds of peace, high triumphs hold,

With store of ladies, whose bright eyes
Rain influence, and judge the prize
Of wit or arms, while both contend
To win her grace whom all commend.
There let Hymen oft appear
In saffron robe, with taper clear,
And pomp, and feast, and revelry,
With mask, and antique pageantry;
Such sights as youthful poets dream
On summer eves by haunted stream
Then to the well-trod stage anon,
If Jonson's learned sock be on,
Or sweetest Shakespeare, Fancy's child,
Warble his native wood-notes wild.

   And ever, against eating cares,
Lap me in soft Lydian airs,
Married to immortal verse,
Such as the meeting soul may pierce
In notes, with many a winding bout
Of linkèd sweetness long drawn out,
With wanton heed, and giddy cunning,
The melting voice through mazes running,
Untwisting all the chains that tie
The hidden soul of harmony;
That Orpheus' self may heave his head
From golden slumber on a bed
Of heap'd Elysian flowers, and hear
Such strains as would have won the ear
Of Pluto to have quite set free
His half-regain'd Eurydice.

   These delights if thou canst give,
Mirth, with thee I mean to live.

JOHN MILTON

Strange Meeting

It seemed that out of battle I escaped
Down some profound dull tunnel, long since scooped
Through granites which titanic wars had groined.
Yet also there encumbered sleepers groaned,
Too fast in thought or death to be bestirred.
Then, as I probed them, one sprang up, and stared
With piteous recognition in fixed eyes,
Lifting distressful hands as if to bless.
And by his smile, I knew that sullen hall,
By his dead smile I knew we stood in Hell.
With a thousand pains that vision's face was grained;
Yet no blood reached there from the upper ground,
And no guns thumped, or down the flues made moan.
'Strange friend,' I said, 'here is no cause to mourn.'
'None,' said the other, 'save the undone years,
The hopelessness. Whatever hope is yours,
Was my life also; I went hunting wild
After the wildest beauty in the world,
Which lies not calm in eyes, or braided hair,
But mocks the steady running of the hour,
And if it grieves, grieves richlier than here.
For by my glee might many men have laughed,
And of my weeping something had been left,
Which must die now. I mean the truth untold,
The pity of war, the pity war distilled.
Now men will go content with what we spoiled.
Or, discontent, boil bloody, and be spilled.
They will be swift with swiftness of the tigress,
None will break ranks, though nations trek from progress.
Courage was mine, and I had mystery,
Wisdom was mine, and I had mastery;
To miss the march of this retreating world
Into vain citadels that are not walled

[105]

Then, when much blood had clogged their chariot-wheels
I would go up and wash them from sweet wells,
Even with truths that lie too deep for taint.
I would have poured my spirit without stint
But not through wounds; not on the cess of war.
Foreheads of men have bled where no wounds were.
I am the enemy you killed, my friend.
I knew you in this dark; for so you frowned
Yesterday through me as you jabbed and killed.
I parried; but my hands were loath and cold.
Let us sleep now. . . .'

WILFRED OWEN

The Song of Wandering Ængus

I WENT out to the hazel wood,
Because a fire was in my head,
And cut and peeled a hazel wand,
And hooked a berry to a thread;
And when white moths were on the wing,
And moth-like stars were flickering out,
I dropped the berry in a stream
And caught a little silver trout.

When I had laid it on the floor
I went to blow the fire aflame,
But something rustled on the floor,
And some one called me by my name:
It had become a glimmering girl
With apple blossom in her hair
Who called me by my name and ran
And faded through the brightening air.

Though I am old with wandering
Through hollow lands and hilly lands,
I will find out where she has gone,
And kiss her lips and take her hands;
And walk among long dappled grass,
And pluck till time and times are done
The silver apples of the moon,
The golden apples of the sun.

W. B. YEATS

'And death shall have no dominion'

AND death shall have no dominion.
Dead men naked they shall be one
With the man in the wind and the west moon;
When their bones are picked clean and the clean bones gone,
They shall have stars at elbow and foot;
Though they go mad they shall be sane,
Though they sink through the sea they shall rise again;
Though lovers be lost love shall not;
And death shall have no dominion.

And death shall have no dominion.
Under the windings of the sea
They lying long shall not die windily;
Twisting on racks when sinews give way,
Strapped to a wheel, yet they shall not break;
Faith in their hands shall snap in two,
And the unicorn evils run them through;
Split all ends up they shan't crack;
And death shall have no dominion.

And death shall have no dominion.
No more may gulls cry at their ears
Or waves break loud on the seashores;
Where blew a flower may a flower no more
Lift its head to the blows of the rain;
Though they be mad and dead as nails,
Heads of the characters hammer through daisies;
Break in the sun till the sun breaks down,
And death shall have no dominion.

DYLAN THOMAS

Ulysses

ಬಎ

IT little profits that an idle king,
By this still hearth, among these barren crags,
Match'd with an aged wife, I mete and dole
Unequal laws unto a savage race,
That hoard, and sleep, and feed, and know not me.
I cannot rest from travel: I will drink
Life to the lees: all times I have enjoy'd
Greatly, have suffer'd greatly, both with those
That loved me, and alone; on shore, and when
Thro' scudding drifts the rainy Hyades
Vext the dim sea: I am become a name;
For always roaming with a hungry heart
Much have I seen and known; cities of men
And manners, climates, councils, governments,
Myself not least, but honour'd of them all;
And drunk delight of battle with my peers,
Far on the ringing plains of windy Troy.
I am a part of all that I have met;
Yet all experience is an arch wherethro'
Gleams that untravell'd world, whose margin fades
For ever and for ever when I move.
How dull it is to pause, to make an end,
To rust unburnish'd, not to shine in use!
As tho' to breathe were life. Life piled on life
Were all too little, and of one to me
Little remains: but every hour is saved
From that eternal silence, something more,
A bringer of new things; and vile it were
For some three suns to store and hoard myself,
And this gray spirit yearning in desire
To follow knowledge like a sinking star,
Beyond the utmost bound of human thought.
   This is my son, mine own Telemachus,
To whom I leave the sceptre and the isle –
Well-loved of me, discerning to fulfil
This labour, by slow prudence to make mild
A rugged people, and thro' soft degrees

Subdue them to the useful and the good.
Most blameless is he, centred in the sphere
Of common duties, decent not to fail
In offices of tenderness, and pay
Meet adoration to my household gods,
When I am gone. He works his work, I mine.
   There lies the port; the vessel puffs her sail:
There gloom the dark broad seas. My mariners,
Souls that have toil'd, and wrought, and thought with me –
That ever with a frolic welcome took
The thunder and the sunshine, and opposed
Free hearts, free foreheads – you and I are old;
Old age hath yet his honour and his toil;
Death closes all: but something ere the end,
Some work of noble note, may yet be done,
Not unbecoming men that strove with Gods.
The lights begin to twinkle from the rocks:
The long day wanes: the slow moon climbs: the deep
Moans round with many voices. Come, my friends,
'Tis not too late to seek a newer world.
Push off, and sitting well in order smite
The sounding furrows; for my purpose holds
To sail beyond the sunset, and the baths
Of all the western stars, until I die.
It may be that the gulfs will wash us down:
It may be we shall touch the Happy Isles,
And see the great Achilles, whom we knew.
Tho' much is taken, much abides; and tho'
We are not now that strength which in old days
Moved earth and heaven; that which we are, we are;
One equal temper of heroic hearts,
Made weak by time and fate, but strong in will
To strive, to seek, to find, and not to yield.

ALFRED, LORD TENNYSON

Piano

Softly, in the dusk, a woman is singing to me;
Taking me back down the vista of years, till I see
A child sitting under the piano, in the boom of the tingling strings
And pressing the small, poised feet of a mother who smiles as she
     sings.
In spite of myself, the insidious mastery of song
Betrays me back, till the heart of me weeps to belong
To the old Sunday evenings at home, with winter outside
And hymns in the cosy parlour, the tinkling piano our guide.
So now it is vain for the singer to burst into clamour
With the great black piano appassionato. The glamour
Of childish days is upon me, my manhood is cast
Down in the flood of remembrance, I weep like a child for the past.

D. H. Lawrence

Fern Hill

Now as I was young and easy under the apple boughs
About the lilting house and happy as the grass was green,
    The night above the dingle starry,
      Time let me hail and climb
    Golden in the heydays of his eyes,
And honoured among wagons I was prince of the apple towns
And once below a time I lordly had the trees and leaves
      Trail with daisies and barley
    Down the rivers of the windfall light.

And as I was green and carefree, famous among the barns
About the happy yard and singing as the farm was home,
    In the sun that is young once only,
      Time let me play and be
    Golden in the mercy of his means,
And green and golden I was huntsman and herdsman, the calves
Sang to my horn, the foxes on the hills barked clear and cold,
      And the sabbath rang slowly
    In the pebbles of the holy streams.

All the sun long it was running, it was lovely, the hay
Fields high as the house, the tunes from the chimneys, it was air
    And playing, lovely and watery
      And fire green as grass.
    And nightly under the simple stars
As I rode to sleep the owls were bearing the farm away,
All the moon long I heard, blessed among stables, the night-jars
    Flying with the ricks, and the horses
      Flashing into the dark.

And then to awake, and the farm, like a wanderer white
With the dew, come back, the cock on his shoulder: it was all
    Shining, it was Adam and maiden,
      The sky gathered again
    And the sun grew round that very day.
So it must have been after the birth of the simple light
In the first, spinning place, the spellbound horses walking warm
    Out of the whinnying green stable
      On to the fields of praise.

And honoured among foxes and pheasants by the gay house
Under the new made clouds and happy as the heart was long,
    In the sun born over and over,
        I ran my heedless ways,
    My wishes raced through the house high hay
And nothing I cared, at my sky blue trades, that time allows
In all his tuneful turning so few and such morning songs
    Before the children green and golden
        Follow him out of grace,

Nothing I cared, in the lamb white days, that time would take me
Up to the swallow thronged loft by the shadow of my hand,
    In the moon that is always rising,
        Nor that riding to sleep
    I should hear him fly with the high fields
And wake to the farm forever fled from the childless land.
Oh as I was young and easy in the mercy of his means,
    Time held me green and dying
    Though I sang in my chains like the sea.

DYLAN THOMAS

On first looking into Chapman's Homer

MUCH have I travell'd in the realms of gold,
    And many goodly states and kingdoms seen;
    Round many western islands have I been
Which bards in fealty to Apollo hold.
Oft of one wide expanse had I been told
    That deep-brow'd Homer ruled as his demesne;
    Yet did I never breathe its pure serene
Till I heard Chapman speak out loud and bold:
Then felt I like some watcher of the skies
    When a new planet swims into his ken;
Or like stout Cortez when with eagle eyes
    He star'd at the Pacific – and all his men
Look'd at each other with a wild surmise –
    Silent, upon a peak in Darien.

JOHN KEATS

Sailing to Byzantium

I

THAT is no country for old men. The young
In one another's arms, birds in the trees
– Those dying generations – at their song,
The salmon-falls, the mackerel-crowded seas,
Fish, flesh, or fowl, commend all summer long
Whatever is begotten, born, and dies.
Caught in that sensual music all neglect
Monuments of unageing intellect

II

An aged man is but a paltry thing,
A tattered coat upon a stick, unless
Soul clap its hands and sing, and louder sing
For every tatter in its mortal dress,
Nor is there singing school but studying
Monuments of its own magnificence;
And therefore I have sailed the seas and come
To the holy city of Byzantium.

III

O sages standing in God's holy fire
As in the gold mosaic of a wall,
Come from the holy fire, perne in a gyre,
And be the singing-masters of my soul.
Consume my heart away; sick with desire
And fastened to a dying animal
It knows not what it is; and gather me
Into the artifice of eternity.

IV

Once out of nature I shall never take
My bodily form from any natural thing,
But such a form as Grecian goldsmiths make
Of hammered gold and gold enamelling
To keep a drowsy Emperor awake;
Or set upon a golden bough to sing
To lords and ladies of Byzantium
Of what is past, or passing, or to come.

W. B. YEATS

Song: 'Goe, and catche a falling starre'

GOE, and catche a falling starre,
   Get with child a mandrake roote,
Tell me, where all past yeares are,
   Or who cleft the Divels foot,
Teach me to heare Mermaides singing,
Or to keep off envies stinging,
      And finde
      What winde
Serves to advance an honest minde.

If thou beest borne to strange sights,
   Things invisible to see,
Ride ten thousand daies and nights,
   Till age snow white haires on thee,
Thou, when thou retorn'st, wilt tell mee
All strange wonders that befell thee,
      And sweare
      No where
Lives a woman true, and faire.

If thou findst one, let mee know,
   Such a Pilgrimage were sweet;
Yet doe not, I would not goe,
   Though at next doore wee might meet,
Though shee were true, when you met her,
And last, till you write your letter,
      Yet shee
      Will bee
False, ere I come, to two, or three.

JOHN DONNE

A Valediction: forbidding mourning

As virtuous men passe mildly'away,
    And whisper to their soules, to goe,
Whilst some of their sad friends doe say,
    The breath goes now, and some say, no:

So let us melt, and make no noise,
    No teare-floods, nor sigh-tempests move,
'Twere prophanation of our joyes
    To tell the layetie our love.

Moving of th'earth brings harmes and feares,
    Men reckon what it did and meant,
But trepidation of the spheares
    Though greater farre, is innocent.

Dull sublunary lovers love
    (Whose soule is sense) cannot admit
Absence, because it doth remove
    Those things which elemented it.

But we by'a love, so much refin'd,
    That our selves know not what it is,
Inter-assured of the mind,
    Care less, eyes, lips, and hands to misse.

Our two soules therefore, which are one,
    Though I must goe, endure not yet
A breach, but an expansion,
    Like gold to ayery thinnesse beate.

If they be two, they are two so
    As stiffe twin compasses are two,
Thy soule the fixt foot, makes no show
    To move, but doth, if th'other doe.

And though it in the center sit,
   Yet when the other far doth rome,
It leanes, and hearkens after it,
   And growes erect, as it comes home.

Such wilt thou be to mee, who must
   Like th'other foot, obliquely runne;
Thy firmnes makes my circle just,
   And makes me end, where I begunne.

JOHN DONNE

'The world is too much with us'

THE world is too much with us; late and soon,
Getting and spending, we lay waste our powers
Little we see in Nature that is ours;
We have given our hearts away, a sordid boon!
This Sea that bares her bosom to the moon;
The winds that will be howling at all hours,
And are up-gathered now like sleeping flowers;
For this, for every thing, we are out of tune;
It moves us not. – Great God! I'd rather be
A Pagan suckled in a creed outworn;
So might I, standing on this pleasant lea,
Have glimpses that would make me less forlorn;
Have sight of Proteus rising from the sea;
Or hear old Triton blow his wreathèd horn.

WILLIAM WORDSWORTH

The Listeners

'Is there anybody there?' said the Traveller,
   Knocking on the moonlit door;
And his horse in the silence champed the grasses
   Of the forest's ferny floor:
And a bird flew up out of the turret,
   Above the Traveller's head:
And he smote upon the door a second time;
   'Is there anybody there?' he said.
But no one descended to the Traveller;
   No head from the leaf-fringed sill
Leaned over and looked into his grey eyes,
   Where he stood perplexed and still.
But only a host of phantom listeners
   That dwelt in the lone house then
Stood listening in the quiet of the moonlight
   To that voice from the world of men:
Stood thronging the faint moonbeams on the dark stair,
   That goes down to the empty hall,
Hearkening in an air stirred and shaken
   By the lonely Traveller's call.
And he felt in his heart their strangeness,
   Their stillness answering his cry,
While his horse moved, cropping the dark turf,
   'Neath the starred and leafy sky;
For he suddenly smote on the door, even
   Louder, and lifted his head: –
'Tell them I came, and no one answered,
   That I kept my word,' he said.
Never the least stir made the listeners,
   Though every word he spake
Fell echoing through the shadowiness of the still house
   From the one man left awake:
Ay, they heard his foot upon the stirrup,
   And the sound of iron on stone,
And how the silence surged softly backward,
   When the plunging hoofs were gone.

WALTER DE LA MARE

'Now sleeps the crimson petal, now the white'

Now sleeps the crimson petal, now the white;
Nor waves the cypress in the palace walk;
Nor winks the gold fin in the porphyry font:
The firefly wakens: waken thou with me.

Now droops the milk-white peacock like a ghost,
And like a ghost she glimmers on to me.

Now lies the Earth all Danaë to the stars,
And all thy heart lies open unto me.

Now slides the silent meteor on, and leaves
A shining furrow, as thy thoughts in me.

Now folds the lily all her sweetness up,
And slips into the bosom of the lake:
So fold thyself, my dearest, thou, and slip
Into my bosom and be lost in me.

ALFRED, LORD TENNYSON
from The Princess, VII

Delight in Disorder

A SWEET disorder in the dresse
Kindles in cloathes a wantonnesse:
A Lawne about the shoulders thrown
Into a fine distraction:
An erring Lace, which here and there
Enthralls the Crimson Stomacher:
A Cuffe neglectfull, and thereby
Ribbands to flow confusedly:
A winning wave (deserving Note)
In the tempestuous petticote:
A carelesse shooe-string, in whose tye
I see a wilde civility:
Doe more bewitch me, than when Art
Is too precise in every part.

ROBERT HERRICK

La Figlia Che Piange

O quam te memorem virgo . . .

Stand on the highest pavement of the stair –
Lean on a garden urn –
Weave, weave the sunlight in your hair –
Clasp your flowers to you with a pained surprise –
Fling them to the ground and turn
With a fugitive resentment in your eyes:
But weave, weave the sunlight in your hair.

So I would have had him leave,
So I would have had her stand and grieve,
So he would have left
As the soul leaves the body torn and bruised,
As the mind deserts the body it has used.
I should find
Some way incomparably light and deft,
Some way we both should understand,
Simple and faithless as a smile and shake of the hand.

She turned away, but with the autumn weather
Compelled my imagination many days,
Many days and many hours:
Her hair over her arms and her arms full of flowers.
And I wonder how they should have been together!
I should have lost a gesture and a pose.
Sometimes these cogitations still amaze
The troubled midnight and the noon's repose.

                                                T. S. Eliot

Home Thoughts, from Abroad

O TO be in England
Now that April's there,
And whoever wakes in England
Sees, some morning, unaware,
That the lowest boughs and the brushwood sheaf
Round the elm-tree bole are in tiny leaf,
While the chaffinch sings on the orchard bough
In England – now!

And after April, when May follows,
And the whitethroat builds, and all the swallows!
Hark, where my blossom'd pear-tree in the hedge
Leans to the field and scatters on the clover
Blossoms and dewdrops – at the bent spray's edge –
That's the wise thrush; he sings each song twice over
Lest you should think he never could recapture
The first fine careless rapture!
And though the fields look rough with hoary dew,
All will be gay when noontide wakes anew
The buttercups, the little children's dower
– Far brighter than this gaudy melon-flower!

ROBERT BROWNING

Not Waving but Drowning

NOBODY heard him, the dead man,
But still he lay moaning:
I was much further out than you thought
And not waving but drowning.

Poor chap, he always loved larking
And now he's dead
It must have been too cold for him his heart gave way,
They said.

Oh, no no no, it was too cold always
(Still the dead one lay moaning)
I was much too far out all my life
And not waving but drowning.

STEVIE SMITH

The Walrus and the Carpenter

THE sun was shining on the sea,
  Shining with all his might!
He did his very best to make
  The billows smooth and bright –
And this was odd, because it was
  The middle of the night.

The moon was shining sulkily,
  Because she thought the sun
Had got no business to be there
  After the day was done –
'It's very rude of him,' she said,
  'To come and spoil the fun!'

The sea was wet as wet could be,
  The sands were dry as dry.
You could not see a cloud, because
  No cloud was in the sky:
No birds were flying overhead –
  There were no birds to fly.

The Walrus and the Carpenter
  Were walking close at hand:
They wept like anything to see
  Such quantities of sand:
'If this were only cleared away,'
  They said, 'it would be grand!'

'If seven maids with seven mops
  Swept it for half a year,
Do you suppose,' the Walrus said,
  'That they could get it clear?'
'I doubt it,' said the Carpenter,
  And shed a bitter tear.

'O Oysters, come and walk with us!'
  The Walrus did beseech.
'A pleasant walk, a pleasant talk,
  Along the briny beach:
We cannot do with more than four,
  To give a hand to each.'

The eldest Oyster looked at him,
　　But never a word he said:
The eldest Oyster winked his eye,
　　And shook his heavy head –
Meaning to say he did not choose
　　To leave the oyster-bed.

But four young Oysters hurried up,
　　All eager for the treat:
Their coats were brushed, their faces washed,
　　Their shoes were clean and neat –
And this was odd, because, you know,
　　They hadn't any feet.

Four other Oysters followed them,
　　And yet another four;
And thick and fast they came at last,
　　And more, and more, and more –
All hopping through the frothy waves,
　　And scrambling to the shore.

The Walrus and the Carpenter
　　Walked on a mile or so,
And then they rested on a rock
　　Conveniently low:
And all the little Oysters stood
　　And waited in a row.

'The time has come,' the Walrus said,
　　'To talk of many things:
Of shoes – and ships – and sealing-wax –
　　Of cabbages – and kings –
And why the sea is boiling hot –
　　And whether pigs have wings.'

'But wait a bit,' the Oysters cried,
　　'Before we have our chat;
For some of us are out of breath,
　　And all of us are fat!'
'No hurry!' said the Carpenter.
　　They thanked him much for that.

'A loaf of bread,' the Walrus said,
  'Is what we chiefly need:
Pepper and vinegar besides
  Are very good indeed –
Now, if you're ready, Oysters dear,
  We can begin to feed.'

'But not on us!' the Oysters cried,
  Turning a little blue.
'After such kindness, that would be
  A dismal thing to do!'
'The night is fine,' the Walrus said.
  'Do you admire the view?

'It was so kind of you to come!
  And you are very nice!'
The Carpenter said nothing but
  'Cut us another slice.
I wish you were not quite so deaf –
  I've had to ask you twice!'

'It seems a shame,' the Walrus said,
  'To play them such a trick.
After we've brought them out so far,
  And made them trot so quick!'
The Carpenter said nothing but
  'The butter's spread too thick!'

'I weep for you,' the Walrus said·
  'I deeply sympathise.'
With sobs and tears he sorted out
  Those of the largest size,
Holding his pocket-handkerchief
  Before his streaming eyes.

'O Oysters,' said the Carpenter,
  'You've had a pleasant run!
Shall we be trotting home again!'
  But answer came there none –
And this was scarcely odd, because
  They'd eaten every one.

                    LEWIS CARROLL

An Arundel Tomb

SIDE by side, their faces blurred,
The earl and countess lie in stone,
Their proper habits vaguely shown
As jointed armour, stiffened pleat,
And that faint hint of the absurd –
The little dogs under their feet.

Such plainness of the pre-baroque
Hardly involves the eye, until
It meets his left-hand gauntlet, still
Clasped empty in the other; and
One sees, with a sharp tender shock,
His hand withdrawn, holding her hand.

They would not think to lie so long.
Such faithfulness in effigy
Was just a detail friends would see:
A sculptor's sweet commissioned grace
Thrown off in helping to prolong
The Latin names around the base.

They would not guess how early in
Their supine stationary voyage
The air would change to soundless damage,
Turn the old tenantry away;
How soon succeeding eyes begin
To look, not read. Rigidly they

Persisted, linked, through lengths and breadths
Of time. Snow fell, undated. Light
Each summer thronged the glass. A bright
Litter of birdcalls strewed the same
Bone-riddled ground. And up the paths
The endless altered people came,

Washing at their identity.
Now, helpless in the hollow of
An unarmorial age, a trough,
Of smoke in slow suspended skeins
Above their scrap of history,
Only an attitude remains:

Time has transfigured them into
Untruth. The stone fidelity
They hardly meant has come to be
Their final blazon, and to prove
Our almost-instinct almost true:
What will survive of us is love.

PHILIP LARKIN

The Donkey

WHEN fishes flew and forests walked
    And figs grew upon thorn,
Some moment when the moon was blood
    Then surely I was born;

With monstrous head and sickening cry
    And ears like errant wings,
The devil's walking parody
    On all four-footed things.

The tattered outlaw of the earth,
    Of ancient crooked will;
Starve, scourge, deride me: I am dumb,
    I keep my secret still.

Fools! For I also had my hour;
    One far fierce hour and sweet:
There was a shout about my ears,
    And palms before my feet.

G. K. CHESTERTON

In Memory of Eva Gore-Booth and Con Markiewicz

THE light of evening, Lissadell,
Great windows, open to the south,
Two girls in silk kimonos, both
Beautiful, one a gazelle.
But a raving autumn shears
Blossom from the summer's wreath;
The older is condemned to death,
Pardoned, drags out lonely years
Conspiring among the ignorant.
I know not what the younger dreams –
Some vague Utopia – and she seems,
When withered old and skeleton-gaunt,
An image of such politics.
Many a time I think to seek
One or the other out and speak
Of that old Georgian mansion, mix
Pictures of the mind, recall
That table and the talk of youth,
Two girls in silk kimonos, both
Beautiful, one a gazelle.

Dear shadows, now you know it all,
All the folly of a fight
With a common wrong or right.
The innocent and the beautiful
Have no enemy but time;
Arise and bid me strike a match
And strike another till time catch;
Should the conflagration climb,
Run till all the sages know.
We the great gazebo built,
They convicted us of guilt;
Bid me strike a match and blow.

W. B. YEATS
October 1927

Ode on a Grecian Urn

Thou still unravish'd bride of quietness,
　Thou foster-child of silence and slow time,
Sylvan historian, who canst thus express
　A flowery tale more sweetly than our rhyme:
What leaf-fring'd legend haunts about thy shape
　Of deities or mortals, or of both,
　　In Tempe or the dales of Arcady?
What men or gods are these? What maidens loth?
　What mad pursuit? What struggle to escape?
　　What pipes and timbrels? What wild ecstasy?

Heard melodies are sweet, but those unheard
　Are sweeter; therefore, ye soft pipes, play on;
Not to the sensual ear, but, more endear'd,
　Pipe to the spirit ditties of no tone:
Fair youth, beneath the trees, thou canst not leave
　Thy song, nor ever can those trees be bare;
　　Bold Lover, never, never canst thou kiss,
Though winning near the goal – yet, do not grieve;
　She cannot fade, though thou hast not thy bliss,
　　For ever wilt thou love, and she be fair!

Ah, happy, happy boughs! that cannot shed
　Your leaves, nor ever bid the Spring adieu;
And, happy melodist, unwearied,
　For ever piping songs for ever new;
More happy love! more happy, happy love!
　For ever warm and still to be enjoy'd,
　　For ever panting, and for ever young;
All breathing human passion far above,
　That leaves a heart high-sorrowful and cloy'd,
　　A burning forehead, and a parching tongue.

Who are these coming to the sacrifice?
　To what green altar, O mysterious priest,
Lead'st thou that heifer lowing at the skies,
　And all her silken flanks with garlands drest?
What little town by river or sea shore,

Or mountain-built with peaceful citadel,
　　Is emptied of this folk, this pious morn?
And, little town, thy streets for evermore
　Will silent be; and not a soul to tell
　　Why thou art desolate, can e'er return.
O Attic shape! Fair attitude! with brede
　Of marble men and maidens overwrought,
With forest branches and the trodden weed;
　Thou, silent form, dost tease us out of thought
As doth eternity: Cold Pastoral!
　When old age shall this generation waste,
　　Thou shalt remain, in midst of other woe
Than ours, a friend to man, to whom thou say'st,
　'Beauty is truth, truth beauty,' – that is all
　　Ye know on earth, and all ye need to know.

JOHN KEATS

[135]

'The lowest trees have tops'

THE lowest trees have tops, the ant her gall,
The fly her spleen, the little spark his heat;
The slender hairs cast shadows, though but small,
And bees have stings, although they be not great;
    Seas have their source, and so have shallow springs:
    And love is love, in beggars and in kings.

Where waters smoothest run, there deepest are the fords;
The dial stirs, yet none perceives it move;
The firmest faith is found in fewest words;
The turtles do not sing, and yet they love;
    True hearts have ears and eyes, no tongues to speak:
    They hear and see, and sigh, and then they break.

SIR EDWARD DYER

The Lake Isle of Innisfree

I WILL arise and go now, and go to Innisfree,
And a small cabin build there, of clay and wattles made:
Nine bean-rows will I have there, a hive for the honey-bee,
And live alone in the bee-loud glade.

And I shall have some peace there, for peace comes dropping slow,
Dropping from the veils of the morning to where the cricket sings;
There midnight's all a glimmer, and noon a purple glow,
And evening full of the linnet's wings.

I will arise and go now, for always night and day
I hear lake water lapping with low sounds by the shore;
While I stand on the roadway, or on the pavements grey,
I hear it in the deep heart's core.

W. B. YEATS

Adlestrop

ᘏᕒᘏ

YES. I remember Adlestrop –
The name, because one afternoon
Of heat the express-train drew up there
Unwontedly. It was late June.

The steam hissed. Someone cleared his throat.
No one left and no one came
On the bare platform. What I saw
Was Adlestrop – only the name

And willows, willow-herb, and grass,
And meadowsweet, and haycocks dry,
No whit less still and lonely fair
Than the high cloudlets in the sky.

And for that minute a blackbird sang
Close by, and round him, mistier,
Farther and farther, all the birds
Of Oxfordshire and Gloucestershire.

EDWARD THOMAS

from *Morte d'Arthur*

THEN saw they how there hove a dusky barge,
Dark as a funeral scarf from stem to stern,
Beneath them; and descending they were ware
That all the decks were dense with stately forms
Black-stoled, black-hooded, like a dream – by these
Three Queens with crowns of gold – and from them rose
A cry that shiver'd to the tingling stars,
And, as it were one voice, an agony
Of lamentation, like a wind, that shrills
All night in a waste land, where no one comes,
Or hath come, since the making of the world.
    Then murmur'd Arthur, 'Place me in the barge,'
And to the barge they came. There those three Queens
Put forth their hands, and took the King, and wept.
But she, that rose the tallest of them all
And fairest, laid his head upon her lap,
And loosed the shatter'd casque, and chafed his hands,
And call'd him by his name, complaining loud,
And dropping bitter tears against his brow
Striped with dark blood: for all his face was white
And colourless, and like the wither'd moon
Smote by the fresh beam of the springing east;
And all his greaves and cuisses dash'd with drops
Of onset; and the light and lustrous curls –
That made his forehead like a rising sun
High from the dais-throne – were parch'd with dust;
Or, clotted into points and hanging loose,
Mix'd with the knightly growth that fringed his lips.
So like a shatter'd column lay the King;
Not like that Arthur who, with lance in rest,
From spur to plume a star of tournament,
Shot thro' the lists at Camelot, and charged
Before the eyes of ladies and of kings.

ALFRED, LORD TENNYSON

[139]

The Revenge,
A Ballad of the Fleet

At Flores in the Azores Sir Richard Grenville lay,
And a pinnace, like a flutter'd bird, came flying from far away:
'Spanish ships of war at sea! We have sighted fifty-three!'
Then sware Lord Thomas Howard: ''Fore God I am no coward;
But I cannot meet them here, for my ships are out of gear,
And the half my men are sick. I must fly, but follow quick.
We are six ships of the line; can we fight with fifty-three?'

Then spake Sir Richard Grenville: 'I know you are no coward;
You fly them for a moment to fight with them again.
But I've ninety men and more that are lying sick ashore.
I should count myself the coward if I left them, my Lord Howard,
To these Inquisition dogs and the devildoms of Spain.'

So Lord Howard passed away with five ships of war that day,
Till he melted like a cloud in the silent summer heaven;
But Sir Richard bore in hand all his sick men from the land
Very carefully and slow,
Men of Bideford in Devon,
And we laid them on the ballast down below;
For we brought them all aboard,
And they blessed him in their pain, that they were not left to Spain,
To the thumbscrew and the stake, for the glory of the Lord.

He had only a hundred seamen to work the ship and to fight,
And he sailed away from Flores till the Spaniard came in sight,
With his huge sea-castles heaving upon the weather bow.
'Shall we fight or shall we fly?
Good Sir Richard, tell us now,
For to fight is but to die!
There'll be little of us left by the time this sun be set.'
And Sir Richard said again: 'We be all good English men.
Let us bang these dogs of Seville, the children of the devil,
For I never turn'd my back upon Don or devil yet.'

Sir Richard spoke and he laugh'd, and we roared a hurrah, and so
The little Revenge ran on sheer into the heart of the foe,
With her hundred fighters on deck, and her ninety sick below;
For half of their fleet to the right and half to the left were seen,
And the little Revenge ran on thro' the long sea-lane between.

Thousands of their soldiers look'd down from their decks and laugh'd,
Thousands of their seamen made mock at the mad little craft
Running on and on, till delay'd
By their mountain-like San Philip that, of fifteen hundred tons,
And up-shadowing high above us with her yawning tiers of guns,
Took the breath from our sails, and we stay'd.

And while now the great San Philip hung above us like a cloud
Whence the thunderbolt will fall
Long and loud,
Four galleons drew away
From the Spanish fleet that day,
And two upon the larboard and two upon the starboard lay,
And the battle-thunder broke from them all.

But anon the great San Philip, she bethought herself and went
Having that within her womb that had left her ill content;
And the rest they came aboard us, and they fought us hand to hand,
For a dozen times they came with their pikes and musqueteers,
And a dozen times we shook 'em off as a dog that shakes his ears
When he leaps from the water to the land.

And the sun went down, and the stars came out far over the summer
    sea,
But never a moment ceased the fight of the one and the fifty-three.
Ship after ship, the whole night long, their high-built galleons came,
Ship after ship, the whole night long, with her battle-thunder and
    flame;
Ship after ship, the whole night long, drew back with her dead and her
    shame.
For some were sunk and many were shattered, and so could fight us no
    more –
God of battles, was ever a battle like this in the world before?

[141]

For he said 'Fight on! fight on!'
Though his vessel was all but a wreck;
And it chanc'd, that when half of the short summer night was gone,
With a grisly wound to be drest he had left the deck,
But a bullet struck him that was dressing it suddenly dead,
And himself he was wounded again in the side and the head,
And he said 'Fight on! fight on!'

And the night went down, and the sun smiled out far over the summer
    sea,
And the Spanish fleet with broken sides lay round us all in a ring;
But they dared not touch us again, for they fear'd that we still could
    sting,
So they watch'd what the end would be.
And we had not fought them in vain,
But in perilous plight were we,
Seeing forty of our poor hundred were slain,
And half of the rest of us maim'd for life
In the crash of the cannonades and the desperate strife;
And the sick men down in the hold were most of them stark and cold,
And the pikes were all broken or bent, and the powder was all of it
    spent;
And the masts and the rigging were lying over the side;
But Sir Richard cried in his English pride,
'We have fought such a fight for a day and a night
As may never be fought again!
We have won great glory, my men!
And a day less or more,
At sea or ashore,
We die – does it matter when?
Sink me the ship, Master Gunner, sink her, split her in twain!
Fall into the hands of God, not into the hands of Spain!'

And the gunner said 'Ay, ay,' but the seamen made reply:
'We have children, we have wives,
And the Lord hath spared our lives.
We will make the Spaniard promise, if we yield, to let us go;
We shall live to fight again and to strike another blow.'
And the lion there lay dying, and they yielded to the foe.

And the stately Spanish men to their flagship bore him then,
Where they laid him by the mast, old Sir Richard caught at last,
And they praised him to his face with their courtly foreign grace;
But he rose upon their decks and he cried:
'I have fought for Queen and Faith like a valiant man and true;
I have only done my duty as a man is bound to do.
With a joyful spirit I Sir Richard Grenville die!'
And he fell upon their decks, and he died.

And they stared at the dead that had been so valiant and true,
And had holden the power and glory of Spain so cheap
That he dared her with one little ship and his English few;
Was he devil or man? He was devil for aught they knew,
But they sank his body with honour down into the deep,
And they manned the Revenge with a swarthier, alien crew,
And away she sail'd with her loss and long'd for her own;
When a wind from the lands they had ruin'd awoke from sleep,
And the water began to heave and the weather to moan,
And or ever that evening ended a great gale blew,
And a wave like the wave that is raised by an earthquake grew,
Till it smote on their hulls and their sails and their masts and their flags,
And the whole sea plunged and fell on the shot-shatter'd navy of
   Spain,
And the little Revenge herself went down by the island crags
To be lost evermore in the main.

ALFRED, LORD TENNYSON

The Children's Hour

ಬಿ

Between the dark and the daylight,
    When the night is beginning to lower,
Comes a pause in the day's occupations,
    That is known as the Children's Hour.

I hear in the chamber above me
    The patter of little feet,
The sound of a door that is opened,
    And voices soft and sweet.

From my study I see in the lamplight,
    Descending the broad hall stair,
Grave Alice, and laughing Allegra,
    And Edith with golden hair.

A whisper, and then a silence:
    Yet I know by their merry eyes
They are plotting and planning together
    To take me by surprise.

A sudden rush from the stairway,
    A sudden raid from the hall!
By three doors left unguarded
    They enter my castle wall!

They climb up into my turret
    O'er the arms and back of my chair;
If I try to escape, they surround me;
    They seem to be everywhere.

They almost devour me with kisses,
    Their arms about me entwine,
Till I think of the Bishop of Bingen
    In his Mouse-Tower on the Rhine!

Do you think, O blue-eyed banditti,
    Because you have scaled the wall,
Such an old mustache as I am
    Is not a match for you all!

I have you fast in my fortress,
　And will not let you depart,
But put you down into the dungeon
　In the round-tower of my heart.

And there will I keep you forever,
　Yes, forever and a day,
Till the walls shall crumble to ruin,
　And moulder in dust away!

H. W. LONGFELLOW

Here Live Your Life Out!

WINDOW-gazing, at one time or another
In the course of travel, you must have startled at
Some coign of true felicity. 'Stay!' it beckoned,
'Here live your life out!' If you were simple-hearted
The village rose, perhaps, from a broad stream
Lined with alders and gold-flowering flags –
Hills, mills, hay-fields, orchards – and, plain to see,
The very house behind its mulberry-tree
Stood, by a miracle, untenanted!

Alas, you could not alight, found yourself jolted
Viciously on. Public conveyances
Are not amenable to casual halts
Except in sternly drawn emergencies –
Bandits, floods, landslides, earthquakes or the like –
Nor could you muster resolution enough
To shout: 'This is emergency, let me out!'
Rushing to grasp their brakes; so the whole scene
Withdrew for ever. Once at the terminus
(As your internal mentor will have told you),
It would have been pure folly to engage
A private car, drive back, sue for possession.
Too far, too late:
Already bolder tenants were at the gate.

ROBERT GRAVES

Holy Willie's Prayer

O THOU, wha in the Heavens dost dwell,
Wha, as it pleases best thysel',
Sends ane to heaven and ten to hell,
    A' for thy glory,
And no for ony guid or ill
    They've done afore thee!

I bless and praise thy matchless might,
Whan thousands thou hast left in night,
That I am here afore thy sight,
    For gifts an' grace
A burnin' an' a shinin' light,
    To a' this place.

What was I, or my generation,
That I should get sic exaltation?
I, wha deserve most just damnation,
    For broken laws,
Sax thousand years 'fore my creation,
    Thro' Adam's cause.

When frae my mither's womb I fell,
Thou might hae plungèd me in hell,
To gnash my gums, to weep and wail,
    In burnin' lakes,
Where damnèd devils roar and yell,
    Chain'd to their stakes;

Yet I am here a chosen sample,
To show thy grace is great and ample;
I'm here a pillar in thy temple,
    Strong as a rock,
A guide, a buckler, an example
    To a' thy flock.

O Lord, thou kens what zeal I bear,
When drinkers drink, and swearers swear,
And singin' there and dancin' here,
    Wi' great an' sma':
For I am keepit by thy fear
    Free frae them a'.

But yet, O Lord! confess I must
At times I'm fash'd wi' fleshly lust;
An' sometimes too, in warldly trust,
      Vile self gets in;
But thou remembers we are dust,
      Defil'd in sin.

O Lord! yestreen, thou kens, wi' Meg –
Thy pardon I sincerely beg;
O! may 't ne'er be a livin' plague
      To my dishonour,
An' I'll ne'er lift a lawless leg
      Again upon her.

Besides I farther maun allow,
Wi' Lizzie's lass, three times I trow –
But, Lord, that Friday I was fou,
      When I cam near her,
Or else thou kens thy servant true
      Wad never steer her.

May be thou lets this fleshly thorn
Beset thy servant e'en and morn
Lest he owre high and proud should turn,
      That he's sae gifted;
If sae, thy hand maun e'en be borne
      Until thou lift it.

Lord, bless thy chosen in this place,
For here thou hast a chosen race;
But God confound their stubborn face,
      And blast their name,
Wha bring thy elders to disgrace
      An' public shame.

Lord, mind Gawn Hamilton's deserts,
He drinks, an' swears, an' plays at cartes,
Yet has sae mony takin' arts
      Wi' grit an' sma',
Frae God's ain priest the people's hearts
      He steals awa'.

An' when we chasten'd him therefor,
Thou kens how he bred sic a splore

As set the warld in a roar
   O' laughin' at us;
Curse thou his basket and his store,
   Kail and potatoes.

Lord, hear my earnest cry an' pray'r,
Against that presbyt'ry o' Ayr;
Thy strong right hand, Lord, make it bare
   Upo' their heads;
Lord, weigh it down, and dinna spare,
   For their misdeeds.

O Lord my God, that glib-tongu'd Aiken,
My very heart and soul are quakin',
To think how we stood sweatin', shakin',
   An' piss'd wi' dread,
While he, wi' hingin' lips and snakin',
   Held up his head.

Lord, in the day of vengeance try him,
Lord, visit them wha did employ him,
And pass not in thy mercy by them,
   Nor hear their pray'r:
But, for thy people's sake, destroy them,
   And dinna spare.

But, Lord, remember me and mine
Wi' mercies temp'ral and divine,
That I for gear and grace may shine
   Excell'd by nane,
And a' the glory shall be thine,
   Amen, Amen!

ROBERT BURNS

from *The Hunting of the Snark*

🙟🙝

'JUST the place for a Snark!' the Bellman cried,
    As he landed his crew with care;
Supporting each man on the top of the tide
    By a finger entwined in his hair.

'Just the place for a Snark! I have said it twice:
    That alone should encourage the crew.
Just the place for a Snark! I have said it thrice:
    What I tell you three times is true.'

The crew was complete: it included a Boots –
    A maker of Bonnets and Hoods –
A Barrister, brought to arrange their disputes –
    And a Broker, to value their goods.

A Billiard-marker, whose skill was immense,
    Might perhaps have won more than his share –
But a Banker, engaged at enormous expense,
    Had the whole of their cash in his care.

There was also a Beaver, that paced on the deck,
    Or would sit making lace in the bow:
And had often (the Bellman said) saved them from wreck,
    Though none of the sailors knew how.

There was one who was famed for the number of things
    He forgot when he entered the ship:
His umbrella, his watch, all his jewels and rings,
    And the clothes he had bought for the trip.

He had forty-two boxes, all carefully packed,
    With his name painted clearly on each:
But, since he omitted to mention the fact,
    They were all left behind on the beach.

The loss of his clothes hardly mattered, because
    He had seven coats on when he came,
With three pair of boots – but the worst of it was,
    He had wholly forgotten his name.

He would answer to 'Hi!' or to any loud cry,
    Such as 'Fry me!' or 'Fritter my wig!'
To 'What-you-may-call-um!' or 'What-was-his-name!'
    But especially 'Thing-um-a-jig!'

While, for those who preferred a more forcible word,
    He had different names from these:
His intimate friends called him 'Candle-ends',
    And his enemies 'Toasted-cheese'.

'His form is ungainly – his intellect small –'
    (So the Bellman would often remark)
'But his courage is perfect! And that, after all,
    Is the thing that one needs with a Snark.'

He would joke with hyænas, returning their stare
    With an impudent wag of the head:
And he once went a walk, paw-in-paw, with a bear,
    'Just to keep up its spirits,' he said.

He came as a Baker: but owned, when too late –
    And it drove the poor Bellman half-mad –
He could only bake Bridecake – for which, I may state,
    No materials were to be had.

The last of the crew needs especial remark,
    Though he looked an incredible dunce:
He had just one idea – but, that one being 'Snark',
    The good Bellman engaged him at once.

He came as a Butcher: but gravely declared,
    When the ship had been sailing a week,
He could only kill Beavers. The Bellman looked scared,
    And was almost too frightened to speak:

But at length he explained, in a tremulous tone,
    There was only one Beaver on board;
And that was a tame one he had of his own,
    Whose death would he deeply deplored.

The Beaver, who happened to hear the remark,
    Protested, with tears in its eyes,
That not even the rapture of hunting the Snark
    Could atone for that dismal surprise!

It strongly advised that the Butcher should be
  Conveyed in a separate ship:
But the Bellman declared that would never agree
  With the plans he had made for the trip;

Navigation was always a difficult art,
  Though with only one ship and one bell:
And he feared he must really decline, for his part,
  Undertaking another as well.

The Beaver's best course was, no doubt, to procure
  A second-hand dagger-proof coat –
So the Baker advised it – and next, to insure
  Its life in some Office of note:

This the Banker suggested, and offered for hire
  (On moderate terms), or for sale,
Two excellent Policies, one Against Fire,
  And one Against Damage From Hail.

Yet still, ever after that sorrowful day,
  Whenever the Butcher was by,
The Beaver kept looking the opposite way,
  And appeared unaccountably shy.

LEWIS CARROLL

Non Sum Qualis Eram Bonae Sub Regno Cynarae

Last night, ah, yesternight, betwixt her lips and mine
There fell thy shadow, Cynara! thy breath was shed
Upon my soul between the kisses and the wine;
And I was desolate and sick of an old passion,
    Yea, I was desolate and bowed my head:
I have been faithful to thee, Cynara! in my fashion.

All night upon mine heart I felt her warm heart beat,
Night-long within mine arms in love and sleep she lay;
Surely the kisses of her bought red mouth were sweet;
But I was desolate and sick of an old passion,
    When I awoke and found the dawn was gray;
I have been faithful to thee, Cynara! in my fashion.

I have forgot much, Cynara! gone with the wind,
Flung roses, roses riotously with the throng,
Dancing, to put thy pale, lost lilies out of mind;
But I was desolate and sick of an old passion,
    Yea, all the time, because the dance was long:
I have been faithful to thee, Cynara! in my fashion.

I cried for madder music and for stronger wine,
But when the feast is finished and the lamps expire,
Then falls thy shadow, Cynara! the night is thine;
And I am desolate and sick of an old passion,
    Yea, hungry for the lips of my desire:
I have been faithful to thee, Cynara! in my fashion.

Ernest Dowson

'Our revels now are ended'

Our revels now are ended. These our actors,
As I foretold you, were all spirits and
Are melted into air, into thin air;
And, like the baseless fabric of this vision,
The cloud-capped tow'rs, the gorgeous palaces,
The solemn temples, the great globe itself,
Yea, all which it inherit, shall dissolve,
And, like this insubstantial pageant faded,
Leave not a rack behind. We are such stuff
As dreams are made on, and our little life
Is rounded with a sleep.

WILLIAM SHAKESPEARE
from The Tempest, IV i.

The Pasture

꿍

I'M going out to clean the pasture spring;
I'll only stop to rake the leaves away
(And wait to watch the water clear, I may):
I sha'n't be gone long. – You come too.

I'm going out to fetch the little calf
That's standing by the mother. It's so young
It totters when she licks it with her tongue.
I sha'n't be gone long. – You come too.

ROBERT FROST

'Prithee go in thyself'

PRITHEE go in thyself; seek thine own ease.
This tempest will not give me leave to ponder
On things would hurt me more, but I'll go in.
In, boy; go first. You houseless poverty –
Nay, get thee in. I'll pray, and then I'll sleep.
Poor naked wretches, wheresoe'er you are,
That bide the pelting of this pitiless storm,
How shall your houseless heads and unfed sides,
Your looped and windowed raggedness, defend you
From seasons such as these? O, I have ta'en
Too little care of this! Take physic, pomp;
Expose thyself to feel what wretches feel,
That thou mayst shake the superflux to them
And show the heavens more just.

WILLIAM SHAKESPEARE
from King Lear, III.iv

Psalm 23

THE Lord is my shepherd;
I shall not want.
He maketh me to lie down in green pastures;
He leadeth me beside the still waters.
He restoreth my soul:
He leadeth me in the paths of righteousness
For his name's sake.

Yea, though I walk through the valley of the shadow of death,
I will fear no evil:
For thou art with me;
Thy rod and thy staff, they comfort me.

Thou preparest a table before me
In the presence of mine enemies;
Thou anointest my head with oil;
My cup runneth over.

Surely goodness and mercy shall follow me
All the days of my life:
And I will dwell in the house of the Lord
For ever.

AUTHORISED VERSION OF THE BIBLE

The Relic

𝕠𝕫

WHEN my grave is broke up again
Some second guest to entertain,
(For graves have learn'd that woman-head
To be to more than one a Bed)
And he that digs it, spies
A bracelet of bright haire about the bone,
Will he not let'us alone,
And thinke that there a loving couple lies,
Who thought that this device might be some way
To make their soules, at the last busie day,
Meet at this grave, and make a little stay?

If this fall in a time, or land,
Where mis-devotion doth command,
Then, he that digges us up, will bring
Us, to the Bishop, and the King,
To make us Reliques; then
Thou shalt be'a Mary Magdalen, and I
A something else thereby;
All women shall adore us, and some men;
And since at such times, miracles are sought,
I would that age were by this paper taught
What miracles wee harmeless lovers wrought.

First, we lov'd well and faithfully,
Yet knew not what we lov'd, nor why,
Difference of sex no more we knew,
Than our Guardian Angells doe;
Comming and going, we
Perchance might kisse, but not between those meales;
Our hands ne'er toucht the seales,
Which nature, injur'd by late law, sets free:
These miracles we did; but now alas,
All measure, and all language, I should passe,
Should I tell what a miracle she was.

JOHN DONNE

[158]

from *The Revolution*

I

Not yet had History's Ætna smoked the skies,
And low the Gallic Giantess lay enchained,
While overhead in ordered set and rise,
Her kingly crowns immutably defiled;
Effulgent on funereal piled
Across the vacant heavens, and distrained
Her body, mutely, even as earth, to bear;
Despoiled the tomb of hope, her mouth of air.

II

Through marching scores of winters racked she lay,
Deneath a hoar-frost's brilliant crust;
Whereon the jewelled flies that drained
Her breasts disported in a glistering spray;
She, the land's fount of fruits, enclosed with dust;
By good and evil angels fed, sustained
In part to curse, in part to pray,
Sucking the dubious rumours, till men saw
The throbs of her charged heart before the Just,
So worn the harrowed surface had become:
And still they deemed the dance above was Law,
Amort all passion in a rebel dumb.

III

Then on the unanticipated day,
Earth heaved, and rose a veinous mound
To roar of the underfloods; and off it sprang,
Ravishing as red wine in woman's form,
A splendid Mænad, she of the delirious laugh,
Her body twisted flames with the smoke-cap crowned;
She of the Bacchic foot; the challenger to the fray,
Bewitchment for the embrace; who sang, who sang
Intoxication to her swarm,
Revolved them, hair, voice, feet, in her carmagnole,
As with a stroke she snapped the Royal staff,

Dealt the awaited blow on gilt decay
(O ripeness of the time! O Retribution sure,
If but our vital lamp illume us to endure!)
And, like a glad releasing of her soul,
Sent the word Liberty up to meet the midway blue,
Her bridegroom in descent to her; and they joined,
In the face of men they joined: attest it true,
The million witnesses, that she
For ages lying beside the mole,
Was on the unanticipated miracle day
Upraised to midway heaven and, as to her goal
Enfolded, ere the Immaculate knew
What Lucifer of the Mint had coined
His bride's adulterate currency
Of burning love corrupt of an infuriate hate;
She worthy, she unworthy; that one day his mate:
His mate for that one day of the unwritten deed.
Read backward on the hoar-frost's brilliant crust;
Beneath it read.
Athirst to kiss, athirst to slay, she stood.
A radiance fringed with grim affright;
For them that hungered, she was nourishing food,
For those who sparkled, Night.
Read in her heart, and how before the Just
Her doings, her misdoings, plead.

IV

Down on her leap for him the young Angelical broke
To husband a resurgent France:
From whom, with her dethroning stroke,
Dishonour passed; the dalliance,
That is occasion's yea or nay,
In issues for the soul to pay,
Discarded; and the cleft 'twixt deed and word,
The sinuous lie which warbles the sweet bird,
Wherein we see old Darkness peer,
Cold Dissolution beck, she had flung hence;
And hence the talons and the beak of prey;
Hence all the lures to silken swine
Thronging the troughs of indolence;
With every sleek convolvement serpentine;
The pride in elfin arts to veil an evil leer,

And bid a goatfoot trip it like a fay.
He clasped in this revived, uprisen France,
A valorous dame, of countenance
The lightning's upon cloud: unlit as yet
On brows and lips the lurid shine
Of seas in the night-wind's whirl; unstirred
Her pouch of the centuries' injuries compressed;
The shriek that tore the world as yet unheard:
Earth's animate full flower she looked, intense
For worship, wholly given him, fair
Adoring or desiring; in her bright jet,
Earth's crystal spring to sky: Earth's warrior Best
To win Heaven's Pure up that midway
We vision for new ground, where sense
And spirit are one for the further flight; breast-bare,
Bare-limbed; nor graceless gleamed her disarray
In scorn of the seductive insincere,
But martially nude for hot Bellona's play,
And amorous of the loftiest in her view.

V

She sprang from dust to drink of earth's cool dew,
The breath of swaying grasses share,
Mankind embrace, their weaklings rear,
At wrestle with the tyrannic strong;
Her forehead clear to her mate, virgin anew,
As immortals may be in the mortal sphere.
Read through her launching heart, who had lain long
With Earth and heard till it became her own,
Our good Great Mother's eve and matin song:
The humming burden of Earth's toil to feed
Her creatures all, her task to speed their growth,
Her aim to lead them up her pathways, shown
Between the Pains and Pleasures; warned of both,
Of either aided on their hard ascent.
Now when she looked with love's benign delight
After great ecstasy, along the plains,
What foulest impregnation of her sight
Transformed the scene to multitudinous troops
Of human sketches, quaver-figures, bent,
As were they winter sedges, broken hoops,
Dry udders, vineless poles, worm-eaten posts,

[161]

With features like the flowers defaced by deluge rains?
Recked she that some perverting devil had limned
Earth's proudest to spout scorn of the Maker's hand,
Who could a day behold these deathly hosts.
And see, decked, graced, and delicately trimmed
A ribanded and gemmed elected few,
Sanctioned, of milk and honey starve the land: –
Like melody in flesh, its pleasant game
Olympianwise perform, cloak but the shame:
Beautiful statures; hideous,
By Christian contrast; pranked with golden chains,
And flexile where is manhood straight;
Mortuaries where warm should beat
The brotherhood that keeps blood sweet:
Who dared in cantique impious
Proclaim the Just, to whom was due
Cathedral gratitude in the pomp of state,
For that on those lean outcasts hung the sucker Pains,
On these elect the swelling Pleasures grew.
Surely a devil's land when that meant death for each!
Fresh from the breast of Earth, not thus,
With all the body's life to plump the leech,
Is Nature's way, she knew. The abominable scene
Spat at the skies; and through her veins,
To cloud celestially sown,
Ran venom of what nourishment
Her dark sustainer subterrene
Supplied her, stretched supine on the rack,
Alive in the shrewd nerves, the seething brains,
Under derisive revels, prone
As one clamped fast, with the interminable senseless blent.

GEORGE MEREDITH

The Solitary Reaper

BEHOLD her, single in the field,
　　Yon solitary Highland Lass!
Reaping and singing by herself;
　　Stop here, or gently pass!
Alone she cuts and binds the grain,
And sings a melancholy strain;
Oh, listen! for the Vale profound
Is overflowing with the sound.

No Nightingale did ever chaunt
　　More welcome notes to weary bands
Of travellers in some shady haunt,
　　Among Arabian sands:
A voice so thrilling ne'er was heard
In spring-time from the Cuckoo-bird,
Breaking the silence of the seas
Among the farthest Hebrides.

Will no one tell me what she sings? –
　　Perhaps the plaintive numbers flow
For old, unhappy, far-off things,
　　And battles long ago:
Or is it some more humble lay,
Familiar matter of to-day?
Some natural sorrow, loss, or pain,
That has been, and may be again?

Whate'er the theme, the Maiden sang
　　As if her song could have no ending:
I saw her singing at her work,
　　And o'er the sickle bending; –
I listen'd, motionless and still;
And, as I mounted up the hill,
The music in my heart I bore,
Long after it was heard no more.

WILLIAM WORDSWORTH

The Thousandth Man

ONE man in a thousand, Solomon says,
Will stick more close than a brother.
And it's worth while seeking him half your days
If you find him before the other.
Nine hundred and ninety-nine depend
On what the world sees in you,
But the Thousandth Man will stand your friend
With the whole round world agin you.

'Tis neither promise nor prayer nor show
Will settle the finding for 'ee.
Nine hundred and ninety-nine of 'em go
By your looks, or your acts, or your glory.
But if he finds you and you find him,
The rest of the world don't matter;
For the Thousandth Man will sink or swim
With you in any water.

You can use his purse with no more talk
Than he uses yours for his spendings,
And laugh and meet in your daily walk
As though there had been no lendings.
Nine hundred and ninety-nine of 'em call
For silver and gold in their dealings;
But the Thousandth Man he's worth 'em all,
Because you can show him your feelings.

His wrong's your wrong, and his right's your right,
In season or out of season.
Stand up and back it in all men's sight –
With *that* for your only reason!
Nine hundred and ninety-nine can't bide
The shame or mocking or laughter,
But the Thousandth Man will stand by your side
To the gallows-foot – and after!

RUDYARD KIPLING

[164]

Myfanwy

KIND o'er the *kinderbank* leans my Myfanwy,
   White o'er the play-pen the sheen of her dress,
Fresh from the bathroom and soft in the nursery
   Soap-scented fingers I long to caress.

Were you a prefect and head of your dormit'ry?
   Were you a hockey girl, tennis or gym?
Who was your favourite? Who had a crush on you?
   Which were the baths where they taught you to swim?

Smooth down the Avenue glitters the bicycle,
   Black-stockinged legs under navy-blue serge,
Home and Colonial, Star, International,
   Balancing bicycle leant on the verge

Trace me your wheel-tracks, you fortunate bicycle,
   Out of the shopping and into the dark,
Back down the Avenue, back to the pottingshed,
   Back to the house on the fringe of the park.

Golden the light on the locks of Myfanwy,
   Golden the light on the book on her knee,
Finger-marked pages of Rackham's Hans Andersen,
   Time for the children to come down to tea.

Oh! Fuller's angel-cake, Robertson's marmalade,
   Liberty lampshade, come, shine on us all,
My! what a spread for the friends of Myfanwy
   Some in the alcove and some in the hall.

Then what sardines in the half-lighted passages!
   Locking of fingers in long hide-and-seek.
You will protect me, my silken Myfanwy,
   Ringleader, tom-boy, and chum to the weak.

SIR JOHN BETJEMAN

The Lost Leader

Just for a handful of silver he left us,
  Just for a riband to stick in his coat –
Found the one gift of which fortune bereft us,
  Lost all the others she lets us devote;
They, with the gold to give, doled him out silver,
  So much was theirs who so little allowed;
How all our copper had gone for his service!
  Rags – were they purple, his heart had been proud!
We that had loved him so, followed him, honoured him,
  Lived in his mild and magnificent eye,
Learned his great language, caught his clear accents,
  Made him our pattern to live and to die!
Shakespeare was of us, Milton was for us,
  Burns, Shelley, were with us – they watch from their graves!
He alone breaks from the van and the freemen,
  He alone sinks to the rear and the slaves!

We shall march prospering, – not thro' his presence;
  Songs may inspirit us, – not from his lyre;
Deeds will be done, – while he boasts his quiescence,
  Still bidding crouch whom the rest bade aspire:
Blot out his name, then, record one lost soul more,
  One task more declined, one more footpath untrod,
One more triumph for devils and sorrow for angels,
  One wrong more to man, one more insult to God!
Life's night begins: let him never come back to us!
  There would be doubt, hesitation and pain,
Forced praise on our part – the glimmer of twilight,
  Never glad confident morning again!
Best fight on well, for we taught him, – strike gallantly,
  Menace our heart ere we master his own;
Then let him receive the new knowledge and wait us,
  Pardoned in Heaven, the first by the throne!

ROBERT BROWNING

from *Don Juan, III*

THE isles of Greece! the isles of Greece!
  Where burning Sappho loved and sung,
Where grew the arts of war and peace,
  Where Delos rose, and Phoebus sprung!
Eternal summer gilds them yet,
But all, except their sun, is set.

The Scian and the Teian muse,
  The hero's harp, the lover's lute,
Have found the fame your shores refuse:
  Their place of birth alone is mute
To sounds which echo further west
Than your sires' 'Islands of the Blest'.

The mountains look on Marathon –
  And Marathon looks on the sea;
And musing there an hour alone,
  I dream'd that Greece might still be free;
For standing on the Persians' grave,
I could not deem myself a slave.

A king sate on the rocky brow
  Which looks o'er sea-born Salamis;
And ships, by thousands, lay below,
  And men in nations; – all were his!
He counted them at break of day –
And when the sun set, where were they?

And where are they? and where art thou,
  My country? On thy voiceless shore
The heroic lay is tuneless now –
  The heroic bosom beats no more!
And must thy lyre, so long divine,
Degenerate into hands like mine?

'Tis something in the dearth of fame,
  Though link'd among a fetter'd race,
To feel at least a patriot's shame,
  Even as I sing, suffuse my face;
For what is left the poet here?
For Greeks a blush – for Greece a tear.

Must *we* but weep o'er days more blest?
  Must *we* but blush? – Our fathers bled.
Earth! render back from out thy breast
  A remnant of our Spartan dead!
Of the three hundred grant but three,
To make a new Thermopylae!

What, silent still? and silent all?
  Ah! no; – the voices of the dead
Sound like a distant torrent's fall,
  And answer, 'Let one living head,
But one, arise, – we come, we come!'
'Tis but the living who are dumb.

In vain – in vain: strike other chords;
  Fill high the cup with Samian wine!
Leave battles to the Turkish hordes,
  And shed the blood of Scio's vine!
Hark! rising to the ignoble call –
How answers each bold Bacchanal!

You have the Pyrrhic dance as yet;
  Where is the Pyrrhic phalanx gone?
Of two such lessons, why forget
  The nobler and the manlier one?
You have the letters Cadmus gave –
Think ye he meant them for a slave?

Fill high the bowl with Samian wine!
  We will not think of themes like these!
It made Anacreon's song divine:
  He served – but served Polycrates –
A tyrant; but our masters then
Were still, at least, our countrymen.

The tyrant of the Chersonese
  Was freedom's best and bravest friend;
That tyrant was Miltiades!
  O that the present hour would lend
Another despot of the kind!
Such chains as his were sure to bind.

Fill high the bowl with Samian wine!
  On Suli's rock, and Parga's shore,
Exists the remnant of a line

[168]

Such as the Doric mothers bore;
And there, perhaps, some seed is sown,
The Heracleidan blood might own.

Trust not for freedom to the Franks –
    They have a king who buys and sells;
In native swords and native ranks
    The only hope of courage dwells:
But Turkish force and Latin fraud
Would break your shield, however broad.

Fill high the bowl with Samian wine!
    Our virgins dance beneath the shade –
I see their glorious black eyes shine;
    But gazing on each glowing maid,
My own the burning tear-drop laves,
To think such breasts must suckle slaves.

Place me on Sunium's marbled steep,
    Where nothing, save the waves and I,
May hear our mutual murmurs sweep;
    There, swan-like, let me sing and die:
And land of slaves shall ne'er be mine –
Dash down yon cup of Samian wine!

LORD BYRON
from Don Juan, III

from *The Prologue to the Canterbury Tales*

WHEN April with his showers sweet
The drought of March has pierced to the root,
And bathed every vein in such liquor,
Of whose virtue is engendered the flower;
When Zephyr too with his sweet breath
Has made alive in every grove and field
The tender sprouts, and the young sun
Has in the Ram his half course run,
And small birds make melody
That sleep all night with open eye –
So Nature goads them in their hearts –
Then people long to go on pilgrimages,
And palmers to seek strange shores
To far-off shrines, known in various lands;
And specially from every shires' end
Of England, to Canterbury they wend,
The holy blessed martyr to seek
Who helped them when they were sick.

It happened that, in that season on a day,
In Southwark, at the Tabard as I lay,
Ready to travel on my pilgrimage
To Canterbury with a fully devout heart,
At night there came into that inn
Full nine and twenty in a company
Of sundry folk, by chance fallen
Into fellowship, and pilgrims were they all
That toward Canterbury would ride.
The chambers and the stables were large,
And well were we treated with the best.
In brief, when the sun had gone to rest,
I had so spoken with them, every one,
That I was forthwith of their fellowship,
And made an agreement to rise early
And take our way, as I shall tell you.

GEOFFREY CHAUCER

Kubla Khan

IN Xanadu did Kubla Khan
   A stately pleasure-dome decree;
Where Alph, the sacred river, ran
Through caverns measureless to man
   Down to a sunless sea.

So twice five miles of fertile ground
With walls and towers were girdled round;
And here were gardens bright with sinuous rills
Where blossomed many an incense-bearing tree;
And here were forests ancient as the hills,
Enfolding sunny spots of greenery.

But O, that deep romantic chasm which slanted
Down the green hill athwart a cedarn cover!
A savage place! as holy and enchanted
As e'er beneath a waning moon was haunted
By woman wailing for her demon-lover!
And from this chasm, with ceaseless turmoil seething,
As if this earth in fast thick pants were breathing,
A mighty fountain momently was forced;
Amid whose swift half-intermitted burst
Huge fragments vaulted like rebounding hail,
Or chaffy grain beneath the thresher's flail:
And 'mid these dancing rocks at once and ever:
It flung up momently the sacred river.
Five miles meandering with a mazy motion
Through wood and dale the sacred river ran,
Then reached the caverns measureless to man,
And sank in tumult to a lifeless ocean:
And 'mid this tumult Kubla heard from far
Ancestral voices prophesying war!

   The shadow of the dome of pleasure
   Floated midway on the waves;
   Where was heard the mingled measure
   From the fountain and the caves.
It was a miracle of rare device,
A sunny pleasure-dome with caves of ice!

A damsel with a dulcimer
In a vision once I saw:
It was an Abyssinian maid,
And on her dulcimer she played,
Singing of Mount Abora.
Could I revive within me
Her sympathy and song,
To such a deep delight 'twould win me,
That with music loud and long,
I would build that dome in air,
That sunny dome! those caves of ice!
And all who heard should see them there,
And all should cry, Beware! Beware!
His flashing eyes, his floating hair!
Weave a circle round him thrice,
And close your eyes with holy dread,
For he on honey-dew hath fed,
And drunk the milk of Paradise.

SAMUEL TAYLOR COLERIDGE

Moonlit Apples

AT the top of the house the apples are laid in rows,
And the skylight lets the moonlight in, and those
Apples are deep-sea apples of green. There goes
   A cloud on the moon in the autumn night.

A mouse in the wainscot scratches, and scratches, and then
There is no sound at the top of the house of men
Or mice; and the cloud is blown, and the moon again
   Dapples the apples with deep-sea light.

They are lying in rows there, under the gloomy beams;
On the sagging floor; they gather the silver streams
Out of the moon, those moonlit apples of dreams,
   And quiet is the steep stair under.

In the corridors under there is nothing but sleep.
And stiller than ever on orchard boughs they keep
Tryst with the moon, and deep is the silence, deep
   On moon-washed apples of wonder.

JOHN DRINKWATER

The Hollow Men

A penny for the Old Guy

===

I

WE are the hollow men
We are the stuffed men
Leaning together
Headpiece filled with straw. Alas!
Our dried voices, when
We whisper together
Are quiet and meaningless
As wind in dry grass
Or rats' feet over broken glass
In our dry cellar

Shape without form, shade without colour,
Paralysed force, gesture without motion;

Those who have crossed
With direct eyes, to death's other Kingdom
Remember us – if at all – not as lost
Violent souls, but only
As the hollow men
The stuffed men.

II

Eyes I dare not meet in dreams
In death's dream kingdom
These do not appear:
There, the eyes are
Sunlight on a broken column
There, is a tree swinging
And voices are
In the wind's singing
More distant and more solemn
Than a fading star.

Let me be no nearer
In death's dream kingdom
Let me also wear

Such deliberate disguises
Rat's coat, crowskin, crossed staves
In a field
Behaving as the wind behaves
No nearer –

Not that final meeting
In the twilight kingdom

III

This is the dead land
This is cactus land
Here the stone images
Are raised, here they receive
The supplication of a dead man's hand
Under the twinkle of a fading star.

Is it like this
In death's other kingdom
Waking alone
At the hour when we are
Trembling with tenderness
Lips that would kiss
Form prayers to broken stone.

IV

The eyes are not here
There are no eyes here
In this valley of dying stars
In this hollow valley
This broken jaw of our lost kingdoms

In this last of meeting places
We grope together
And avoid speech
Gathered on this beach of the tumid river

Sightless, unless
The eyes reappear
As the perpetual star
Multifoliate rose
Of death's twilight kingdom
The hope only
Of empty men.

V

Here we go round the prickly pear
Prickly pear prickly pear
Here we go round the prickly pear
At five o'clock in the morning.

Between the idea
And the reality
Between the motion
And the act
Falls the Shadow

                    For Thine is the Kingdom

Between the conception
And the creation
Between the emotion
And the response
Falls the Shadow

                    Life is very long

Between the desire
And the spasm
Between the potency
And the existence
Between the essence
And the descent
Falls the Shadow

                    For Thine is the Kingdom

For Thine is
Life is
For Thine is the

This is the way the world ends
This is the way the world ends
This is the way the world ends
Not with a bang but a whimper.

                        T. S. ELIOT

The Road not Taken

ಎಲ

Two roads diverged in a yellow wood,
And sorry I could not travel both
And be one traveller, long I stood
And looked down one as far as I could
To where it bent in the undergrowth;

Then took the other, as just as fair,
And having perhaps the better claim,
Because it was grassy and wanted wear;
Though as for that the passing there
Had worn them really about the same,

And both that morning equally lay
In leaves no step had trodden black.
Oh, I kept the first for another day!
Yet knowing how way leads on to way,
I doubted if I should ever come back.

I shall be telling this with a sigh
Somewhere ages and ages hence:
Two roads diverged in a wood, and I –
I took the one less travelled by,
And that has made all the difference.

ROBERT FROST

The Collar

I STRUCK the board, and cry'd, No more.
        I will abroad.
    What? shall I ever sigh and pine?
My lines and life are free; free as the rode,
        Loose as the winde, as large as store.
            Shall I be still in suit?
        Have I no harvest but a thorn
        To let me bloud, and not restore
        What I have lost with cordiall fruit?
            Sure there was wine
Before my sighs did drie it: there was corn
        Before my tears did drown it.
        Is the yeare onely lost to me?
            Have I no bayes to crown it?
No flowers, no garlands gay? all blasted?
            All wasted?
        Not so, my heart: but there is fruit,
            And thou hast hands.
        Recover all thy sigh-blown age
On double pleasures: leave thy cold dispute
Of what is fit, and not. Forsake thy cage,
            Thy rope of sands,
Which pettie thoughts have made, and made to thee
        Good cable, to enforce and draw,
            And be thy law,
While thou didst wink and wouldst not see.
            Away; take heed:
            I will abroad.
Call in thy deaths head there: tie up thy fears.
        He that forbears
        To suit and serve his need,
            Deserves his load.
But as I rav'd and grew more fierce and wilde
        At every word,
    Me thought I heard one calling, *Child!*
        And I reply'd, *My Lord.*

GEORGE HERBERT

The Flower

How fresh, O Lord, how sweet and clean
Are thy returns! ev'n as the flowers in spring;
    To which, besides their own demean,
The late-past frosts tributes of pleasure bring.
        Grief melts away
        Like snow in May,
As if there were no such cold thing.

Who would have thought my shrivel'd heart
Could have recover'd greennesse? It was gone
    Quite under ground; as flowers depart
To see their mother-root, when they have blown;
        Where they together
        All the hard weather,
Dead to the world, keep house unknown.

These are thy wonders, Lord of power,
Killing and quickning, bringing down to hell
    And up to heaven in an houre;
Making a chiming of a passing-bell.
        We say amisse,
        This or that is:
Thy word is all, if we could spell.

() that I once past changing were,
Fast in thy Paradise, where no flower can wither!
    Many a spring I shoot up fair,
Offring at heav'n, growing and groning thither:
        Nor doth my flower
        Want a spring-showre,
My sinnes and I joining together.

But while I grow in a straight line,
Still upwards bent, as if heav'n were mine own,
    Thy anger comes, and I decline:
What frost to that? what pole is not the zone,
        Where all things burn,
        When thou dost turn,
And the least frown of thine is shown?

And now in age I bud again,
After so many deaths I live and write;
I once more smell the dew and rain,
And relish versing: O my onely light,
It cannot be
That I am he
On whom they tempests fell all night.

These are thy wonders, Lord of love,
To make us see we are but flowers that glide:
Which when we once can finde and prove,
Thou has a garden for us, where to bide.
Who would be more,
Swelling through store,
Forfeit their Paradise by their pride.

GEORGE HERBERT

Felix Randal

 relx Randal the farrier, O he is dead then? my duty all ended,
Who have watched his mould of man, big-boned and hardy-handsome
Pining, pining, till time when reason rambled in it and some
Fatal four disorders, fleshed there, all contended?

Sickness broke him. Impatient he cursed at first, but mended
Being anointed and all; though a heavenlier heart began some
Months earlier, since I had our sweet reprieve and ransom
Tendered to him Ah well, God rest him all road ever he offended!

This seeing the sick endears them to us, us too it endears.
My tongue had taught thee comfort, touch had quenched thy tears,
Thy tears that touched my heart, child, Felix, poor Felix Randal;

How far from then forethought of, all thy more boisterous years,
When thou at the random grim forge, powerful amidst peers,
Didst fettle for the great grey drayhorse his bright and battering sandal!

Gerard Manley Hopkins

THE CONTRIBUTORS

List of Contributors

Numbers indicate the order in which the contributors listed their chosen poems; an asterisk indicates where the contributors specifically put their poems in no order of preference.

Martin Amis

1	Paradise Lost	John Milton
2	To his Coy Mistress	Andrew Marvell
3	Ulysses	Alfred, Lord Tennyson
4	Sailing to Byzantium	W. B. Yeats
5	The Rime of the Ancient Mariner	Samuel Taylor Coleridge
6	The Love Song of J. Alfred Prufrock	T. S. Eliot
7	'Bright star, would I were steadfast as thou art'	John Keats
8	The Sick Rose	William Blake
9	Strange Meeting	Wilfred Owen
10	Exile's Letter	Ezra Pound

Jeffrey Archer

1	The Thousandth Man	Rudyard Kipling
2	Disabled	Wilfred Owen
3	Under Milk Wood	Dylan Thomas
4	The Whitsun Weddings	Philip Larkin
5	'The world's a stage'	Hilaire Belloc
6	The Old Vicarage, Grantchester	Rupert Brooke
7	In Westminster Abbey	Sir John Betjeman
8	The Burial of Sir John Moore after Corunna	Charles Wolfe
9	Mad Dogs and Englishmen	Noel Coward
10	'How doth the little crocodile'	Lewis Carroll

[184]

Pamela Armstrong

* On Monsieur's Departure	Queen Elizabeth I
'Upon her soothing breast'	Emily Brontë
Maternity	Alice Meynell
'There was a small woman called G . . .'	Anonymous
Nervous Prostration	Anna Wickham
The Battle Hymn of the Republic	Julia Ward Howe
The Second Wife	Lizette Woodworth Reese
Wild Women Blues	Ida Cox
'I think I was enchanted'	Emily Dickinson
Adam Pos'd	Anne Finch, Countess of Winchilsea

Dame Peggy Ashcroft

* Ode: Intimations of Immortality	William Wordsworth
Lycidas	John Milton
The Love Song of J. Alfred Prufrock	T. S. Eliot
The Dong with a Luminous Nose	Edward Lear
'The lowest trees have tops'	Sir Edward Dyer
The Ecstasy	John Donne
'Fear no more the heat o' the sun' (*from* Cymbeline, IV.ii)	William Shakespeare
A Toccata of Galuppi's	Robert Browning
I'm Explaining a Few Things	Pablo Neruda
Afterwards	Thomas Hardy

Beryl Bainbridge

1	Non Sum Qualis Eram	Ernest Dowson
2	Dover Beach	Matthew Arnold
3	'So, we'll go no more a roving'	Lord Byron
4	Little Gidding	T. S. Eliot
5	Sun and Fun: Song of a night-club proprietress	Sir John Betjeman
6	The Highwayman	Alfred Noyes
7	The Lady of Shalott	Alfred, Lord Tennyson
8	The Slave's Dream	H. W. Longfellow

| 9 | The Burial of Sir John Moore after Corunna | Charles Wolfe |
| 10 | If – | Rudyard Kipling |

The Rt Hon Kenneth Baker MP

1	Sonnet 60: 'Like as the waves make towards the pebbled shore'	William Shakespeare
2	The Prologue to the Canterbury Tales	Geoffrey Chaucer
3	L'Allegro	John Milton
4	Bishop Blougram's Apology	Robert Browning
5	Pied Beauty	Gerard Manley Hopkins
6	Tintern Abbey	William Wordsworth
7	The 'Mary Gloster'	Rudyard Kipling
8	The Whitsun Weddings	Philip Larkin
9	Little Gidding	T. S. Eliot
10	The Rape of the Lock	Alexander Pope

Richard Baker OBE

1	Ode to a Nightingale	John Keats
2	Sonnet 116: 'Let me not to the marriage of true minds'	William Shakespeare
3	Sonnet 104: 'To me, fair friend, you never can be old'	William Shakespeare
4	Four Quartets	T. S. Eliot
5	Christmas	Sir John Betjeman
6	Spring Offensive	Wilfred Owen
7	The Autumnal	John Donne
8	To his Coy Mistress	Andrew Marvell
9	At a Solemn Music	John Milton
10	'The world is too much with us'	William Wordsworth

Joan Bakewell

*	The Lie	Sir Walter Raleigh
	Portrait of a Lady	T. S. Eliot
	Villanelle	Harry Guest
	To his Coy Mistress	Andrew Marvell
	Sonnet 110: 'Alas, 'tis true, I have gone here and there'	William Shakespeare
	'Fear no more the heat o' the sun' (*from* Cymbeline, IV.ii)	William Shakespeare

Let Me Die a Young Man's Death	Roger McGough
Not Waving but Drowning	Stevie Smith
Church Going	Philip Larkin
Remembrance	Emily Brontë

The Rt Hon John Biffen MP

1	'When I was one-and-twenty' (*from* A Shropshire Lad, xiii)	A. E. Housman
2	The Lost Leader	Robert Browning
3	I. M. – R. T. Hamilton Bruce	W. E. Henley
4	Fire and Ice	Robert Frost
5	To the Virgins, to make much of Time	Robert Herrick
6	Anthem for Doomed Youth	Wilfred Owen
7	Le Lac	Alphonse Lamartine
8	To his Coy Mistress	Andrew Marvell
9	Ode: Intimations of Immortality	William Wordsworth
10	Autumn	Roy Campbell

Maeve Binchy

1	To Autumn	John Keats
2	Ode to the West Wind	Percy Bysshe Shelley
3	To his Coy Mistress	Andrew Marvell
4	Lays of Ancient Rome	Thomas Babington Macaulay
5	The Song of Hiawatha	H. W. Longfellow
6	L'Allegro	John Milton
7	Il Penseroso	John Milton
8	Tintern Abbey	William Wordsworth
9	My Dark Rosaleen!	J. C. Mangan

Claire Bloom

1	'So, we'll go no more a roving'	Lord Byron
2	Ode on Melancholy	John Keats
3	The Windhover	Gerard Manley Hopkins
4	'Because I could not stop for Death'	Emily Dickinson
5	Man and Wife	Robert Lowell
6	East Coker	T. S. Eliot
7	Leda and the Swan	W. B. Yeats

8	The Lotos–Eaters	Alfred, Lord Tennyson
9	To Sleep	John Keats
10	Ode to a Nightingale	John Keats

Richard Briers

1	The Solitary Reaper	William Wordsworth
2	The Whitsun Weddings	Philip Larkin
3	Jabberwocky	Lewis Carroll
4	Albert and the Lion	Marriott Edgar
5	Gus: the Theatre Cat	T. S. Eliot
6	Death in Leamington	Sir John Betjeman
7	'Now the hungry lion roars' (*from* A Midsummer Night's Dream, V.i)	William Shakespeare
8	The Burning of the Leaves	Laurence Binyon
9	Lines in memoriam regarding the entertainment I gave on 31st of March 1893 in Reform Street Hall, Dundee	William McGonagall
10	'I once was out with Henry in the days/When Henry loved me' (*from* Becket, V.ii)	Alfred, Lord Tennyson

Dora Bryan

*	Daffodils	William Wordsworth
	Renouncement	Alice Meynell
	When I'm Alone	Siegfried Sassoon
	The Question	Percy Bysshe Shelley
	The Walrus and the Carpenter	Lewis Carroll
	Cargoes	John Masefield
	If I Should Ever by Chance	Edward Thomas
	Milk for the Cat	Harold Monro
	Leisure	W. H. Davies
	Upon Westminster Bridge	William Wordsworth

James Burke

1	The Relic	John Donne
2	The Collar	George Herbert
3	To his Coy Mistress	Andrew Marvell
4	'They flee from me that sometime did me seek'	Sir Thomas Wyatt
5	La Figlia Che Piange	T. S. Eliot

6	Sonnet 30: 'When to the sessions of sweet silent thought'	William Shakespeare
7	'From far, from eve and morning' (*from* A Shropshire Lad, xxxii)	A. E. Housman
8	The Lake Isle of Innisfree	W. B. Yeats
9	My Last Duchess	Robert Browning
10	When You are Old	W. B. Yeats

Sir Alastair Burnet

1	Dover Beach	Matthew Arnold
2	Sonnet 18: 'Shall I compare thee to a summer's day?'	William Shakespeare
3	Ode: Intimations of Immortality	William Wordsworth
4	Ode on a Grecian Urn	John Keats
5	Eheu, fugaces (To Postumus)	Quintus Horatius Flaccus (Horace)
6	'How do I love thee?' (*from* Sonnets from the Portuguese, xliii)	Elizabeth Barrett Browning
7	A Poor Scholar of the Forties	Padraic Colum
8	Adonais	Percy Bysshe Shelley
9	Under Ben Bulben, vi	W. B. Yeats
10	Timor Mortis Conturbat Me	William Dunbar

John Carey

1	To Autumn	John Keats
2	Lycidas	John Milton
3	'A slumber did my spirit seal'	William Wordsworth
4	Tithonus	Alfred, Lord Tennyson
5	The Love Song of J. Alfred Prufrock	T. S. Eliot
6	Sonnet 71: 'No longer mourn for me when I am dead'	William Shakespeare
7	Sailing to Byzantium	W. B. Yeats
8	A Nocturnal upon St Lucy's Day	John Donne
9	An Arundel Tomb	Philip Larkin
10	Lullaby: 'Lay your sleeping head, my love'	W. H. Auden

Catherine Cookson OBE
 1 The Children's Hour   H. W. Longfellow
 2 Sonnet 60: 'Like as the waves   William Shakespeare
    make towards the pebbled
    shore'
 3 The Eve of Waterloo   Lord Byron
 4 In the Dordogne   John Peale Bishop
 5 Cities and Thrones and   Rudyard Kipling
    Powers
 6 Song: 'Goe, and catche a   John Donne
    falling starre'
 7 Verses Written in a Lady's   Earl of Chesterfield
    Sherlock 'Upon Death'
 8 An Elegy on a Lap Dog   John Gay
 9 'Know then thyself, presume   Alexander Pope
    not God to scan' (*from* An
    Essay on Man, II)
10 The Inquest   W. H. Davies

Jilly Cooper
 1 The Rime of the Ancient   Samuel Taylor Coleridge
    Mariner
 2 The Flower   George Herbert
 3 Tintern Abbey   William Wordsworth
 4 To an Adopted Child   Anonymous
 5 Stopping by Woods on a   Robert Frost
    Snowy Evening
 6 Horatius   Thomas Babington Macaulay
 7 Ulysses   Alfred, Lord Tennyson
 8 'Tell me not here, it needs not   A. E. Housman
    saying'
 9 The Galloping Cat   Stevie Smith
10 'Forth goes the woodman,   William Cowper
    leaving unconcerned/The
    cheerful haunts of man'
    (*from* The Task, V)

Cyril Cusack
 1 The Leaden Echo and the   Gerard Manley Hopkins
    Golden Echo
 2 Felix Randal   Gerard Manley Hopkins

3	The Windhover	Gerard Manley Hopkins
4	Sonnet 18: 'Shall I compare thee to a summer's day?'	William Shakespeare
5	In Memory of Eva Gore-Booth and Con Markiewicz	W. B. Yeats
6	Upon Westminster Bridge	William Wordsworth
7	A Christmas Childhood	Patrick Kavanagh
8	La Figlia Che Piange	T. S. Eliot
9	Golden Stockings	Oliver St John Gogarty
10	The O'Rahilly	W. B. Yeats

Tessa Dahl

1	When You are Old	W. B. Yeats
2	The Sunlight on the Garden	Louis MacNeice
3	The Busy Heart	Rupert Brooke
4	'The hand that signed the paper felled a city'	Dylan Thomas
5	The Final Word	Dom Moraes
6	Ghosts	Elizabeth Jennings
7	Another Time	W. H. Auden
8	If I should Learn, in Some Quite Casual Way	Edna St Vincent Millay
9	The Donkey	G. K. Chesterton
10	Uphill	Christina Rossetti

Charles Dance

1	Sonnet 29: 'When, in disgrace with Fortune and men's eyes'	William Shakespeare
2	Kubla Khan	Samuel Taylor Coleridge
3	A Dream in the Luxembourg	Richard Aldington
4	'Do not go gentle into that good night'	Dylan Thomas
5	Ballad of the Spanish Civil Guard	Federico García Lorca
6	Waiting for the Barbarians	C. P. Cavafy
7	The Vulture	Hilaire Belloc
8	Not Waving but Drowning	Stevie Smith
9	Party Piece	Brian Patten
10	The Aesthete (*from* The Bab Ballads)	Sir W. S. Gilbert

Len Deighton
1 The Ballad of Reading Gaol   Oscar Wilde
2 The Hollow Men   T. S. Eliot
3 Exposure   Wilfred Owen
4 Anthem for Doomed Youth   Wilfred Owen
5 Delight in Disorder   Robert Herrick
6 Judging Distances   Henry Reed
7 Harbour Ferry   Roy Fuller
8 Song of the Dying Gunner   Charles Causley
9 Sonnet 29: 'When, in disgrace   William Shakespeare
   with Fortune and men's
   eyes'
10 If –   Rudyard Kipling

Jonathan Dimbleby
1 'Prithee go in thyself' (*from* William Shakespeare
   King Lear, III.iv)
2 Show Saturday   Philip Larkin
3 On First Looking into   John Keats
   Chapman's Homer
4 Clearances (Sonnet 7)   Seamus Heaney
5 An Arundel Tomb   Philip Larkin
6 Two in the Campagna   Robert Browning
7 East Coker   T. S. Eliot
8 Boy at the Window   Richard Wilbur
9 The Hawk in the Rain   Ted Hughes
10 September 1st, 1939   W. H. Auden

Frederick Forsyth
1 The Rubáiyát of Omar   Edward Fitzgerald
   Khayyám
2 The Soldier   Rupert Brooke
3 Ode to a Nightingale   John Keats
4 Elegy Written in a Country   Thomas Gray
   Churchyard
5 The Ballad of Reading Gaol   Oscar Wilde
6 L'Ennui   Charles Baudelaire
7 Sacra Fames   Charles Baudelaire
8 The Burial of Sir John Moore   Charles Wolfe
   after Corunna
9 The Rime of the Ancient   Samuel Taylor Coleridge
   Mariner

| 10 | The Revenge, A Ballad of the Fleet | Alfred, Lord Tennyson |

Dick Francis

1	Under Milk Wood	Dylan Thomas
2	Jim	Hilaire Belloc
3	The Law the Lawyers Know About	H. D. C. Pepler
4	Song: 'For Mercy, Courage, Kindness, Mirth'	Laurence Binyon
5	If –	Rudyard Kipling
6	How they brought the Good News from Ghent to Aix	Robert Browning
7	'Do not go gentle into that good night'	Dylan Thomas

George MacDonald Fraser

*	'When icicles hang by the wall' (from Love's Labour's Lost, V.ii)	William Shakespeare
	'My love is like a red, red rose'	Robert Burns
	The Listeners	Walter de la Mare
	The Crowning of Dreaming John	John Drinkwater
	The Golden Journey to Samarkand	J. E. Flecker
	I Remember, I Remember	Thomas Hood
	The Choice	Dante Gabriel Rossetti
	The Ballad of East and West	Rudyard Kipling
	Captain Stratton's Fancy	John Masefield
	The Rolling English Road	G. K. Chesterton

Fiona Fullerton

1	'How do I love thee?' (from Sonnets from the Portuguese, xliii)	Elizabeth Barrett Browning
2	Halfway Down	A. A. Milne
3	Vespers	A. A. Milne
4	A Thought	A. A. Milne
5	If –	Rudyard Kipling
6	Daffodils	William Wordsworth
7	Morte d'Arthur	Alfred, Lord Tennyson

8	The Walrus and the Carpenter	Lewis Carroll
9	The Pied Piper of Hamelin	Robert Browning
10	The Rime of the Ancient Mariner	Samuel Taylor Coleridge

Liza Goddard

1	The Pasture	Robert Frost
2	The Road not Taken	Robert Frost
3	Hunter Trials	Sir John Betjeman
4	To his Coy Mistress	Andrew Marvell
5	Maud	Alfred, Lord Tennyson
6	Love's Growth	John Donne
7	Lullaby: 'Lay your sleeping head, my love'	W. H. Auden
8	Death of an Actor	Hugo Williams
9	An Ode to the Queen on Her Jubilee Year	William McGonagall
10	Matilda	Hilaire Belloc

The Rt Hon Bryan Gould MP

1	On his Blindness	John Milton
2	Ozymandias	Percy Bysshe Shelley
3	To his Coy Mistress	Andrew Marvell
4	Porphyria's Lover	Robert Browning
5	The Donkey	G. K. Chesterton
6	The Tiger	William Blake
7	Sonnet 18: 'Shall I compare thee to a summer's day?'	William Shakespeare
8	On First Looking into Chapman's Homer	John Keats
9	Oxford: Sudden Illness at the Bus-stop	Sir John Betjeman
10	'My love is like a red, red rose'	Robert Burns

Mike Harding

1	Pied Beauty	Gerard Manley Hopkins
2	The Love Song of J. Alfred Prufrock	T. S. Eliot
3	Exposure	Wilfred Owen
4	The Whitsun Weddings	Philip Larkin
5	North	Seamus Heaney
6	Victor Jara of Chile	Adrian Mitchell

7	The Sun Rising	John Donne
8	'And death shall have no dominion'	Dylan Thomas
9	The Emperor of Ice-Cream	Wallace Stevens
10	Lady Lazarus	Sylvia Plath

The Rt Hon Roy Hattersley MP

1	Dover Beach	Matthew Arnold
2	Sonnet 18: 'Shall I compare thee to a summer's day?'	William Shakespeare
3	Sonnet 29: 'When, in disgrace with Fortune and men's eyes'	William Shakespeare
4	Naming of Parts	Henry Reed
5	A Shropshire Lad	A. E. Housman
6	American Names	Stephen Vincent Benét
7	One Word More	Robert Browning
8	Dockery and Son	Philip Larkin
9	In Memory of Eva Gore-Booth and Con Markiewicz	W. B. Yeats
10	Lycidas	John Milton

Nigel Hawthorne

*	I Remember, I Remember	Philip Larkin
	Sonnet 116: 'Let me not to the marriage of true minds'	William Shakespeare
	Journey of the Magi	T. S. Eliot
	Slough	Sir John Betjeman
	Babi Yar	Yevgeny Yevtushenko
	Coming Round	Christopher Hope
	The Night Mail	W. H. Auden
	The Rime of the Ancient Mariner	Samuel Taylor Coleridge
	Attack	Siegfried Sassoon
	Home Thoughts, from Abroad	Robert Browning

The Rt Hon Denis Healey CH MBE MP

| 1 | Sonnet 73: 'That time of year thou mayst in me behold' | William Shakespeare |
| 2 | The Second Coming | W. B. Yeats |

3	Fern Hill	Dylan Thomas
4	'At the round earth's imagined corners'	John Donne
5	Ode to a Nightingale	John Keats
6	'So, we'll go no more a roving'	Lord Byron
7	'Thou art indeed just, Lord'	Gerard Manley Hopkins
8	The Antiplatonick	John Cleveland
9	Burnt Norton	T. S. Eliot
10	Lullaby: 'Lay your sleeping head, my love'	W. H. Auden

James Herriot OBE

1	Ozymandias	Percy Bysshe Shelley
2	Ode to a Nightingale	John Keats
3	Ode: Intimations of Immortality	William Wordsworth
4	The Old Vicarage, Grantchester	Rupert Brooke
5	The Garden of Proserpine	Algernon Charles Swinburne
6	Invictus	W. E. Henley
7	Epitaph on an Army of Mercenaries	A. E. Housman
8	The Lake Isle of Innisfree	W. B. Yeats
9	Adlestrop	Edward Thomas
10	'My love is like a red, red rose'	Robert Burns

Sir Michael Hordern

1	'Our revels now are ended' (*from* The Tempest, IV.i)	William Shakespeare
2	'The world is too much with us'	William Wordsworth
3	Inversnaid	Gerard Manley Hopkins
4	La Belle Dame sans Merci	John Keats
5	An Epitaph: 'Here lies a most beautiful lady'	Walter de la Mare
6	Jim	Hilaire Belloc
7	At Castle Boterel	Thomas Hardy
8	Adlestrop	Edward Thomas
9	Tarantella	Hilaire Belloc
10	Prayer before Birth	Louis MacNeice

Barry Humphries
1 Here Live Your Life Out!   Robert Graves
2 Moonlit Apples   John Drinkwater
3 To My Daughter   Stephen Spender
4 The Way through the Woods   Rudyard Kipling
5 Piano   D. H. Lawrence
6 Love and the Child   Ruth Pitter
7 Envoi   Anna Wickham

Felicity Kendal
*   A Considered Reply to a   Jonathan Price
      Child
    To his Coy Mistress   Andrew Marvell
    it may not always be so   e. e. cummings
    The Definition of Love   Andrew Marvell
    A Pity. We Were Such a Good   Yehudu Amichai
      Invention
    The Good-Morrow   John Donne
    My Lover   Wendy Cope
    Remembrance   Sir Thomas Wyatt
    Sonnet 18: 'Shall I compare   William Shakespeare
      thee to a summer's day?'
    The Song of Wandering   W. B. Yeats
      Ængus

Glenys Kinnock
1 Strange Meeting   Wilfred Owen
2 The child is not dead   Ingrid Jonker
3 Sonnet 29: 'When, in disgrace   William Shakespeare
      with Fortune and men's
      eyes'
4 A Grammarian's Funeral   Robert Browning
5 'There is a nobler glory' (*from*   Percy Bysshe Shelley
      Queen Mab, V)
6 'Do not go gentle into that   Dylan Thomas
      good night'
7 The River God of the River   Stevie Smith
      Mimram in Hertfordshire
8 The Great Tablecloth   Pablo Neruda
9 Reading Scheme   Wendy Cope
10 Land of my Mothers   Idris Davies

[197]

Sue Lawley

1	Dover Beach	Matthew Arnold
2	The Love Song of J. Alfred Prufrock	T. S. Eliot
3	To Autumn	John Keats
4	Danny Deever	Rudyard Kipling
5	The Good-Morrow	John Donne
6	The Parting	Michael Drayton
7	The Listeners	Walter de la Mare
8	Home Thoughts, from Abroad	Robert Browning
9	Ozymandias	Percy Bysshe Shelley
10	Morte d'Arthur	Alfred, Lord Tennyson

Elizabeth Longford

1	Sonnet 60: 'Like as the waves make towards the pebbled shore'	William Shakespeare
2	Don Juan	Lord Byron
3	Ode to a Nightingale	John Keats
4	Prometheus Unbound	Percy Bysshe Shelley
5	Purgatorio	Dante Alighieri
6	Tiresias	Alfred, Lord Tennyson
7	The Second Coming	W. B. Yeats
8	'To be a pilgrim'	John Bunyan
9	Tintern Abbey	William Wordsworth
10	'Death be not proud, though some have called thee'	John Donne

Ian McKellen

*	The Leaden Echo and the Golden Echo	Gerard Manley Hopkins
	The Ballad of Reading Gaol	Oscar Wilde
	To his Coy Mistress	Andrew Marvell
	An Irish Airman Foresees his Death	W. B. Yeats
	In my Craft or Sullen Art	Dylan Thomas
	Piano	D. H. Lawrence
	Anthem for Doomed Youth	Wilfred Owen
	The Prelude, Book II	William Wordsworth
	Sonnet 20: 'A woman's face with Nature's own hand painted'	William Shakespeare

Anna Massey

1	Sonnet 18: 'Shall I compare thee to a summer's day'	William Shakespeare
2	Sonnet 66: 'Tired with all these, for restful death I cry'	William Shakespeare
3	He Wishes for the Cloths of Heaven	W. B. Yeats
4	The Song of Wandering Ængus	W. B. Yeats
5	The Soldier	Rupert Brooke
6	To Autumn	John Keats
7	On his Blindness	John Milton
8	Delight in Disorder	Robert Herrick
9	Sonnet 12: 'When I do count the clock that tells the time'	William Shakespeare
10	The Love Song of J. Alfred Prufrock	T. S. Eliot

John Julius Norwich

1	A Toccata of Galuppi's	Robert Browning
2	'When the hounds of spring are on winter's traces'	Algernon Charles Swinburne
3	A St Helena Lullaby	Rudyard Kipling
4	'Yet if His Majesty, our sovereign lord' (*from Preparations*)	Anonymous
5	To —: 'One word is too often profaned'	Percy Bysshe Shelley
6	A Valediction: forbidding mourning	John Donne
7	'So, we'll go no more a roving'	Lord Byron
8	Fern Hill	Dylan Thomas
9	'The lowest trees have tops'	Sir Edward Dyer
10	Ode on a Grecian Urn	John Keats

Claire Rayner

*	The Passionate Shepherd to his Love	Christopher Marlowe
	The Nymph's Reply to the Shepherd	Sir Walter Raleigh
	The Metropolitan Railway	Sir John Betjeman

Song: 'Goe, and catche a falling starre'	John Donne
The Good-Morrow	John Donne
Upon Julia's Clothes	Robert Herrick
Upon Westminster Bridge	William Wordsworth
Ode to a Nightingale	John Keats
The Song of Hiawatha	H. W. Longfellow
The Rubáiyát of Omar Khayyám	Edward Fitzgerald

Mike Read

1	The Revolution	George Meredith
2	Myfanwy	Sir John Betjeman
3	The Funeral of Youth: Threnody	Rupert Brooke
4	Indoor Games near Newbury	Sir John Betjeman
5	The Garden	Harold Monro
6	The Old Vicarage, Grantchester	Rupert Brooke
7	Tangerines	Hugo Williams
8	The Waste Land	T. S. Eliot
9	Oxford	Tom Lovatt-Williams
10	L'Envoie	Hilaire Belloc

Beryl Reid

1	'How do I love thee?' (*from* Sonnets from the Portuguese, xliii)	Elizabeth Barrett Browning
2	Solitude	A. A. Milne
3	'My love is like a red, red rose'	Robert Burns
4	King John's Christmas	A. A. Milne
5	Daffodils	William Wordsworth
6	Christmas Day	Spike Milligan
7	'Now sleeps the crimson petal, now the white' (*from* The Princess, VII)	Alfred, Lord Tennyson
8	A Fond Kiss	Robert Burns
9	The Bells of Heaven	Ralph Hodgson
10	The Friend	A. A. Milne

Jack Rosenthal

| 1 | Psalm 23 | Authorised Version of the Bible |
| 2 | To his Coy Mistress | Andrew Marvell |

3 'Tomorrow, and tomorrow,
   and tomorrow' (*from*
   Macbeth, V.v)
4 Dulce Et Decorum Est   Wilfred Owen
5 The Love Song of J. Alfred   T. S. Eliot
   Prufrock
6 Easter 1916   W. B. Yeats
7 Frank Mills (*from* the musical   Jerome Ragni and James Rado
   Hair)
8 The Rime of the Ancient   Samuel Taylor Coleridge
   Mariner
9 London   William Blake
10 The Song of Hiawatha   H. W. Longfellow

Nick Ross
1 Sunlight   Seamus Heaney
2 When You are Old   W. B. Yeats
3 He Wishes for the Cloths of   W. B. Yeats
   Heaven
4 'Dear Bankers, pay the   A. P. Herbert
   undermentioned hounds'
5 'Dear Sir, it is with pleasure A. L. Grove
   that I thank'
6 The Love Song of J. Alfred   T.S. Eliot
   Prufrock
7 Parliament Hill Fields   Sir John Betjeman
8 Naming of Parts   Henry Reed
9 Annus Mirabilis   Philip Larkin
10 Matilda   Hilaire Belloc

Sir Peter Scott CH CBE DSC FRS
1 The Hunting of the Snark   Lewis Carroll
2 Sonnet 30: 'When to the   William Shakespeare
   sessions of sweet silent
   thought'
3 To Autumn   John Keats
4 Skimbleshanks: the Railway T. S. Eliot
   Cat
5 Christmas   E. Hilton Young
6 The Knight Whose Armour A. A. Milne
   didn't Squeak

7	The Revenge, A Ballad of the Fleet	Alfred, Lord Tennyson
8	To a Skylark	Percy Bysshe Shelley
9	In the Public Gardens	Sir John Betjeman
10	Ducks	F. W. Harvey

The Rt Hon David Steel MP

1	Holy Willie's Prayer	Robert Burns
2	'And death shall have no dominion'	Dylan Thomas
3	Dulce Et Decorum Est	Wilfred Owen
4	The Eve of St Agnes	John Keats
5	'So, we'll go no more a roving'	Lord Byron
6	Embro to the Ploy	Robert Garrick
7	Trench Duty	Siegfried Sassoon
8	Tam o'Shanter	Robert Burns
9	'Bright be the place in thy soul'	Lord Byron
10	Man was made to Mourn	Robert Burns

Dorothy Tutin

*	'Fear no more the heat o' the sun' (*from* Cymbeline, IV.ii)	William Shakespeare
	Sonnet 29: 'When, in disgrace with Fortune and men's eyes'	William Shakespeare
	'O mistress mine, where are you roaming' (*from* Twelfth Night, II.iii)	William Shakeaspeare
	Ode to a Nightingale	John Keats
	'When I have fears that I may cease to be'	John Keats
	'The splendour falls on castle walls' (*from* The Princess, IV)	Alfred, Lord Tennyson
	'Now sleeps the crimson petal, now the white' (*from* The Princess, VII)	Alfred, Lord Tennyson
	I Am	John Clare
	'And now I live and now I die'	Chidiock Tichborne
	'Now dawns the invisible'	Emily Brontë

Katharine Whitehorn

Index of Poets

Index of First Lines

Acknowledgements

For permission to reprint certain poems in this anthology, acknowledgement is made to the following:

W.H. Auden's 'Lay your sleeping head, my love' reprinted by permission of Faber & Faber Ltd and Random House, Inc. from *Collected Poems* by W.H. Auden edited by Edward Mendelson; Hilaire Belloc's 'Jim' reprinted by permission of the Peters Fraser & Dunlop Group Ltd; John Betjeman's 'Myfanwy' from John Betjeman's *Collected Poems*, John Murray (Publishers) Ltd; for Walter de la Mare's 'The Listeners', to The Literary Trustees of Walter de la Mare and the Society of Authors as their representative; T.S. Eliot's 'The Love Song of J. Alfred Prufrock', 'La Figlia Che Piange' and 'The Hollow Men' reprinted by permission of Faber & Faber Ltd and Harcourt Brace Jovanovich, Inc. from *Collected Poems 1909–1962* by T.S. Eliot Copyright 1936 by Harcourt Brace Jovanovich, Inc. Copyright 1964, 1963 by T.S. Eliot; Robert Frost's 'The Pasture' and 'The Road not Taken' reprinted by permission of the Estate of Robert Frost, Jonathan Cape Ltd and Henry Holt and Company, Inc. from *The Poetry of Robert Frost* edited by Edward Connery Lathem Copyright 1916, 1939, 1967, 1969 by Holt, Rinehart and Winston, Inc. Copyright 1944 by Robert Frost; Robert Graves's 'Here Live Your Life Out!' reprinted by permission of A.P. Watt Ltd on behalf of The Executors of the Estate of Robert Graves; for Rudyard Kipling's 'If' and 'The Thousandth Man', to Hodder & Stoughton Ltd; Philip Larkin's 'The Whitsun Weddings' and 'An Arundel Tomb' reprinted by permission of Faber & Faber Ltd from *The Whitsun Weddings* by Philip Larkin; D.H. Lawrence's 'Piano' reprinted by permission of Laurence Pollinger Ltd, the Estate of Mrs Frieda Lawrence Ravagli and Viking Penguin, Inc. from *The Complete Poems of D.H. Lawrence* collected & edited by Vivian de Sola Pinto and F. Warren Roberts Copyright 1964, 1971 by Angelo Ravagli and C.M. Weekley, Executors of the Estate of Frieda Lawrence Ravagli; for Wilfred Owen's 'Anthem for Doomed Youth', 'Exposure', 'Dulce Et Decorum Est' and 'Strange Meeting' from *The Poems of Wilfred Owen*, The Hogarth Press, to the Estate of Wilfred Owen; Stevie Smith's 'Not Waving but Drowning' from Stevie Smith's *Not Waving But Drowning*, Andre Deutsch Ltd (1957); Dylan Thomas's 'Do not go gentle into that good night', 'Under Milk Wood' (extract), 'And death shall have no dominion' and 'Fern Hill' from *The Poems* and *Under Milk Wood* (Dent), and *Poems of Dylan Thomas* Copyright 1945 by the Trustees of Dylan Thomas (1952) and *Under Milk Wood* Copyright 1954 by New Directions Publishing Corporation, reprinted by permission of New Directions Publishing Corporation; W.B. Yeats's 'The Second Coming' Copyright 1924 by Macmillan Publishing Company, renewed 1952 by Bertha Georgie Yeats, 'Sailing to Byzantium' Copyright 1928 by Macmillan Publishing Company, renewed 1956 by Georgie Yeats, 'In Memory of Eva Gore-Booth and Con Markiewicz' Copyright 1933 by Macmillan Publishing Company, renewed 1961 by Bertha Georgie Yeats, 'The Song of Wandering Ængus', 'When You are Old' and 'The Lake Isle of Innisfree' reprinted by permission of Macmillan Publishing Company from *The Poems of W.B. Yeats: A New Edition*, edited by Richard J. Finneran, Macmillan, New York (1983).